A Nature Poem for Every Night of the Year

A Nature Poem for Every Night of the Year

BATSFORD

Edited by
Jane McMorland Hunter

First published in the United Kingdom in 2020
This edition first published in the United Kingdom in 2026 by
Batsford
43 Great Ormond Street
London WC1N 3HZ
An imprint of B. T. Batsford Holdings Ltd

ISBN 978 1 83733 046 1

A CIP catalogue record for this book
is available from the British Library.

10 9 8 7 6 5 4 3 2 1

Printed by IMAK Ofset, Turkey
Reproduction by Rival Colour Ltd, UK

This book can be ordered direct from the publisher at
www.batsfordbooks.com, or try your local bookshop

Illustrations by Clare Owen

Distributed throughout the UK and Europe by Abrams & Chronicle Books, 1st Floor, 22–24 Ely Place, London EC1N 6TE and 57 rue Gaston Tessier, 75166 Paris, France.

www.abramsandchronicle.co.uk
info@abramsandchronicle.co.uk

CONTENTS

To Matilda, who came home. And to Mat and Sarah, who helped. With all my love.

ABOUT THE EDITOR

Jane McMorland Hunter has compiled seven anthologies of poetry for Batsford and the National Trust. She also writes gardening and cookery books and works as a gardener and at Hatchards bookshop in Piccadilly. She lives in London with a small, grey tabby cat.

Introduction

It may seem obvious, but everything looks different at night. Shadows take on a deeper hue and colours appear indistinct. Shapes that are harmless in daylight are transformed in the dark of night, becoming menacing or beguiling. This is the realm of the nightingale and the owl, the moon and the stars. I have deliberately avoided the darkest poems but, in more ways than the obvious, the night is darker than the day. Our fears come to the surface and we cannot see what may be lurking beyond the patches of light in the deep shadows. Here you will find some poems of uncertainty, loss, disquiet and enchantment. Midnight, for many poets, is a crucial turning point, more than simply a change of date: ''Tis the hour of endings, ended, / Of beginnings, unbegun.' (Laurence Binyon). With this in mind, some poems in this collection look forward to the dawn whilst others look back to nature in the daylight hours.

Strictly speaking, nature is associated with the wild – the physical world untouched by man. My definition also includes the more domesticated pets and gardens, as well as mythical creatures and enchanted ones. Nature poems are inevitably closely linked with all aspects of human life: the sight of lambs gambolling in the sunshine has the power to lift our spirits, just as the eerie hoot of an owl on a cold winter's night can strike fear in any heart. Early poets ascribed the movement of the seasons and the natural world to God, gods or magical powers and, whilst we now know most things can be explained by science, there is still an unworldly beauty surrounding a host of golden daffodils or a crimson sunset.

Many poems that are not primarily about nature still often briefly paint pictures of the natural world. I have deliberately cut poems to include some of these fleeting glimpses, even if it involves obscuring the true meaning of the poem. Details of the complete poem are given as I hope the reader will be seduced by the extract and seek out the entire work. The opening lines of Samuel Taylor Coleridge's 'Frost at Midnight' are a case in point, as are six lines I have taken from William Wordsworth's 'The Two-Part Prelude'. I have also included poems of friendship, love and loss set within a theme of nature. Robert Browning's 'Meeting' and 'Night' and Henry Wadsworth Longfellow's 'The Tide Rises, the Tide Falls' each tell the story of a journey but their setting earns them both a place in this collection.

My seasons deliberately follow an idealistic cycle. In this imagined world flowers, animals and birds are occasionally caught out by untimely frosts and winds but, on the whole, the seasons arrive and depart as they should. Snow appears punctually in December, falls magically on Christmas Eve and never turns to slush. Thrushes herald the arrival of spring and summer rains fall with perfect timing, providing gentle relief rather than devastating floods. We know where we are, as Amy Lowell says 'For to-morrow Winter drops into the waste-basket, / And the calendar calls it March.'

These poems do not necessarily reflect a realistic view of the world and its climate today but the works of John Clare, George MacDonald, Rachel Field and Emily Dickinson create visions that we can all appreciate and learn from. These poems were not collected to form a manifesto but they all remind us that we must look after nature. Many were written on things that are already lost to us, woe that, through our actions or inactions, we should lose even more. There are no polar ice caps in these verses but birdsong, the sight of stars, fields of wild flowers and dappled woodlands are all endangered. This anthology gives a poem to read for every night of the year, I hope that at least some of them will remind us of the fragility and beauty of Earth.

Good-night; ensured release,
Imperishable peace,
        Have these for yours,
While sea abides, and land,
And earth's foundations stand,
        And heaven endures.

From 'Parta Quies' by A. E. Housman

JANUARY

The Stars were Sparkling Clear

Tapestry Trees

Oak.
I am the Roof-tree and the Keel;
I bridge the seas for woe and weal.

Fir.
High o'er the lordly oak I stand,
And drive him on from land to land.

Ash.
I heft my brother's iron bane;
I shaft the spear, and build the wain.

Yew.
Dark down the windy dale I grow,
The father of the fateful Bow.

Poplar.
The war-shaft and the milking-bowl
I make, and keep the hay-wain whole.

Olive.
The King I bless; the lamps I trim;
In my warm wave do fishes swim.

Apple-tree.
I bowed my head to Adam's will;
The cups of toiling men I fill.

Vine.

I draw the blood from out the earth;
I store the sun for winter mirth.

Orange-tree.

Amidst the greenness of my night,
My odorous lamps hang round and bright.

Fig-tree.

I who am little among trees
In honey-making mate the bees.

Mulberry-tree.

Love's lack hath dyed my berries red:
For Love' attire my leaves are shed.

Pear-tree.

High o'er the mead-flowers' hidden feet
I bear aloft my burden sweet.

Bay.

Look on my leafy boughs, the Crown
Of living song and dead renown!

William Morris (1834–1896)

The Months

January brings the snow,
Makes our feet and fingers glow.

February brings the rain,
Thaws the frozen lake again.

March brings breezes loud and shrill,
Stirs the dancing daffodil.

April brings the primrose sweet,
Scatters daises at our feet.

May brings flocks of pretty lambs,
Skipping by their fleecy dams.

June brings tulips, lilies, roses,
Fills the children's hand with posies.

Hot July brings cooling showers,
Apricots and gillyflowers.

August brings the sheaves of corn,
Then the harvest home is borne.

Warm September brings the fruit,
Sportsmen then begin to shoot.

Fresh October brings the pheasant,
Then to gather nuts is pleasant.

Dull November brings the blast,
Then the leaves are whirling fast.

Chill December brings the sleet,
Blazing fire, and Christmas treat.

Sara Coleridge (1802–1852)

Sonnet: The Human Seasons

Four seasons fill the measure of the year;
  There are four seasons in the mind of man:
He has his lusty Spring, when fancy clear
  Takes in all beauty with an easy span:
He has his Summer, when luxuriously
  Spring's honied cud of youthful thought he loves
To ruminate, and by such dreaming high
  Is nearest unto heaven: quiet coves
His soul has in its Autumn, when his wings
  He furleth close; contented so to look
On mists in idleness – to let fair things
    Pass by unheeded as a threshold brook.
He has his Winter too of pale misfeature,
Or else he would forego his mortal nature.

John Keats (1795–1821)

4 JANUARY

A Dream of Summer

VERSES 1–3

Bland as the morning breath of June
  The southwest breezes play;
And, through its haze, the winter noon
  Seems warm as summer's day.
The snow-plumed Angel of the North
  Has dropped his icy spear;
Again the mossy earth looks forth,
  Again the streams gush clear.

The fox his hillside cell forsakes,
  The muskrat leaves his nook,
The bluebird in the meadow brakes
  Is singing with the brook.
'Bear up, O Mother Nature!' cry
  Bird, breeze, and streamlet free;
'Our winter voices prophesy
  Of summer days to thee!'

So, in those winters of the soul,
  By bitter blasts and drear
O'erswept from Memory's frozen pole,
  Will sunny days appear.
Reviving Hope and Faith, they show
  The soul its living powers,
And how beneath the winter's snow
  Lie germs of summer flowers!

John Greenleaf Whittier (1807–1892)

Sonnet 60

Like as the waves make towards the pebbled shore,
So do our minutes hasten to their end;
Each changing place with that which goes before,
In sequent toil all forwards do contend.
Nativity, once in the main of light,
Crawls to maturity, wherewith being crowned,
Crooked eclipses 'gainst his glory fight,
And Time that gave doth now his gift confound.
Time doth transfix the flourish set on youth
And delves the parallels in beauty's brow,
Feeds on the rarities of nature's truth,
And nothing stands but for his scythe to mow:
  And yet to times in hope my verse shall stand,
  Praising thy worth, despite his cruel hand.

William Shakespeare (1564–1616)

Not So Far as the Forest

VERSE 1

I

That chill is in the air
Which the wise know well, and even have learned to bear.
This joy, I know,
Will soon be under snow.

The sun sets in a cloud
And is not seen.
Beauty, that spoke aloud,
Addresses now only the remembering ear.
The heart begins here
To feed on what has been.

Night falls fast.
Today is in the past.

Blown from the dark hill hither to my door
Three flakes, then four
Arrive, then many more.

Edna St Vincent Millay (1892–1950)

The Night of the Dance

The cold moon hangs to the sky by its horn
   And centres its gaze on me;
The stars, like eyes in reverie,
Their westering as for a while forborne,
   Quiz downward curiously.

Old Robert draws the backbrand in,
   The green logs steam and spit;
The half-awakened sparrows flit
From the riddled thatch; and owls begin
   To whoo from the gable-slit.

Yes; far and nigh things seem to know
   Sweet scenes are impending here;
That all is prepared; that the hour is near
For welcomes, fellowships, and flow
   Of sally, song, and cheer;

That spigots are pulled and viols strung;
   That soon will arise the sound
Of measures trod to tunes renowned;
That She will return in Love's low tongue
   My vows as we wheel around.

Thomas Hardy (1840–1928)

The Lake

On a calm day
The lake
Imagines it is a mirror
And smiles back
At people who pass by
Smiling.

On a breezy day
The lake
Hunches its shoulders
And sends ripples
Scudding across the surface.

On a winter's day
The lake
Hides itself
Under a frozen blanket
And refuses to budge
Until it is warm enough
To come out again.

John Foster (1941–)

Impressions I

LES SILHOUETTES

The sea is flecked with bars of grey
The dull dead wind is out of tune,
And like a withered leaf the moon
Is blown across the stormy bay.

Etched clear upon the pallid sand
The black boat lies: a sailor boy
Clambers aboard in careless joy
With laughing face and gleaming hand.

And overheard the curlews cry,
Where through the dusky upland grass
The young brown-throated reapers pass,
Like silhouettes against the sky.

Oscar Wilde (1854–1900)

Trees

I think that I shall never see
A poem as lovely as a tree.

A tree whose hungry mouth is prest
Against the earth's sweet flowing breast;

A tree that looks at God all day,
And lifts her leafy arms to pray;

A tree that may in Summer wear
A nest of robins in her hair;

Upon whose bosom snow has lain
Who intimately lives with rain.

Poems are made by fools like me,
But only God can make a tree.

Joyce Kilmer (1886–1918)

Sonnet IV: To the Moon

Queen of the silver bow! - by thy pale beam,
  Alone and pensive, I delight to stray,
And watch thy shadow trembling in the stream,
  Or mark the floating clouds that cross thy way.
And while I gaze, thy mild and placid light
  Sheds a soft calm upon my troubled breast;
And oft I think – fair planet of the night,
  That in thy orb, the wretched may have rest:
The sufferers of the earth perhaps may go,
  Released by death – to thy benignant sphere,
And the sad children of despair and woe
  Forget in thee, their cup of sorrow here.
Oh! that I soon may reach thy world serene,
Poor wearied pilgrim – in this toiling scene!

Charlotte Smith (1749–1806)

The King of the Wood

Winter: winter in the woods
Is the bone that was the beauty,
The bough that lives the leaf:
The food supplies sink low
And the hedgehog and badger know the hour is late.

Comes snow – the scouting flakes
Nipping out of the north
Followed by bulky brigades
Falling with formidable lust
On land where evil and warm the weevil sleeps.

Spring: the leaves of the chestnut
Hang in the branches like bats;
Bluebells flood into valleys
Where butterflies dry wet wings
And the cock bird lords it in song on his terrain.

This is the season of primrose,
Woodruff, and anemone –
And the season of caterpillars
Of the mottled umber moth
Fattening ambition in a thousand worlds of plenty.

Summer: welcome the woods
When the air sweats in the sun!
Here is a draught of shade
In a cellar deep and dark
Where barrels are so tall they sway like trees.

Now ants are on the hunt
Each for a swag of syrup –
And the felted beech coccus
Seeks out the straight young tree
To lay the foundation stone of a leaning tower.

Autumn: the sky more blue
Than any flower or crystal:
The yellow and wrinkled face
Of the wood is streaked with wounds
As the catkins of the birches slide to the soil.

Burgled boxes with ermine
Lining drop their conkers
Among loot of acorns for squirrels –
And into the earth descends
The cockchafer beetle's larva to mine a future.

Clifford Dyment (1914–1971)

To Winter

'O Winter! bar thine adamantine doors:
The north is thine; there hast thou built thy dark
Deep-founded habitation. Shake not thy roofs
Nor bend thy pillars with thine iron car.'

He hears me not, but o'er the yawning deep
Rides heavy; his storms are unchain'd, sheathèd
In ribbèd steel; I dare not lift mine eyes;
For he hath rear'd his sceptre o'er the world.

Lo! now the direful monster, whose skin clings
To his strong bones, strides o'er the groaning rocks:
He withers all in silence, and in his hand
Unclothes the earth, and freezes up frail life.

He takes his seat upon the cliffs, - the mariner
Cries in vain. Poor little wretch, that deal'st
With storms! – till heaven smiles, and the monster
Is driv'n yelling to his caves beneath mount Hecla.

William Blake (1757–1827)

At Carbis Bay

FROM *INTERMEZZO: PASTORAL*

Out of the night of the sea,
Out of the turbulent night,
A sharp and hurrying wind
Scourges the waters white:
The terror by night.

Out of the doubtful dark,
Out of the night of the land,
What is it breathes and broods
Hoveringly at hand?
The menace of land.

Out of the night of heaven,
Out of the delicate sky,
Pale and serene the stars
In their silence reply:
The peace of the sky.

Arthur Symons (1865–1945)

Snowdrop

Now is the globe shrunk tight
Round the mouse's dulled wintering heart.
Weasel and crow, as if moulded in brass,
Move through an outer darkness
Not in their right minds,
With the other deaths. She, too, pursues her ends,
Brutal as the stars of this month,
Her pale head heavy as metal.

Ted Hughes (1930–1998)

There's a Certain Slant of Light

There's a certain Slant of light,
Winter Afternoons –
That oppresses, like the Heft
Of Cathedral Tunes –

Heavenly Hurt, it gives us –
We can find no scar,
But internal difference –
Where the Meanings, are –

None may teach it – Any –
'Tis the Seal Despair –
An imperial affliction
Sent us of the Air –

When it comes, the Landscape listens –
Shadows – hold their breath –
When it goes, 'tis like the Distance
On the look of Death –

Emily Dickinson (1830–1886)

Evening by the Sea

VERSES 1–3

It was between the night and day,
  The trees looked very weary – one by one
Against the west they seemed to sway,
  And yet were steady. The sad sun
In a sick doubt of colour lay
  Across the water's belt of dun.

On the weak wind scarce flakes of foam
  There floated, hardly bourne at all
From the rent edge of water – some
  Between slack gusts the wind let fall,
The white brine could not overcome
  That pale grass on the southern wall.

That evening one could always hear
  The sharp hiss of the shingle, rent
As each wave settled heavier,
  The same rough way. This noise was blent
With many sounds that hurt the air
  As the salt sea-wind came and went.

Algernon Charles Swinburne (1837–1909)

Winter with the Gulf Stream

The boughs, the boughs are bare enough
But earth has never felt the snow.
Frost-furred our ivies are and rough

With bills of rime the brambles shew.
The hoarse leaves crawl on hissing ground
Because the sighing wind is low.

But if the rain-blasts be unbound
And from dank feathers wring the drops
The clogged brook runs with choking sound

Kneading the mounded mire that stops
His channel under clammy coats
Of foliage fallen in the copse.

A simple passage of weak notes
Is all the winter bird dare try.
The bugle moon by daylight floats

So glassy white about the sky,
So like a berg of hyaline,
And pencilled blue so daintily,

I never saw her so divine.
But through black branches, rarely drest
In scarves of silky shot and shine,

The webbed and the watery west
Where yonder crimson fireball sits
Looks laid for feasting and for rest.

I see long reefs of violets
In beryl-covered fens so dim,
A gold-water Pactolus frets

Its brindled wharves and yellow brim,
The waxen colours weep and run,
And slendering to his burning rim

Into the flat blue mist the sun
Drops out and all our day is done.

Gerard Manley Hopkins (1844–1889)

19 JANUARY

The Two-Part Prelude

LINES 164–169

The leafless trees and every icy crag
Tinkled like iron; while the distant hills
Into the tumult sent an alien sound
Of melancholy, not unnoticed; while the stars,
Eastward, were sparkling clear, and in the west
The orange sky of evening died away.

William Wordsworth (1770–1850)

Winter Morning

All is so still;
The hill a picture of a hill
With silver kine that glimmer
Now whiter and now dimmer
Through the fog's monochrome,
Painted by Cotman or Old Crome.

Pale in the sky
The winter sun shows a round eye,
That darkens and still brightens;
And all the landscape lightens
Till on the melting meadows
The trees are seen with hard white shadows.

Though in the balk
Ice doubles every lump of chalk
And the frost creeps across
The matted leaves in silver moss,
Here where the grass is dank
The sun weeps on this brightening bank.

Andrew Young (1885–1971)

January Dusk

Austere and clad in sombre robes of grey,
  With hands upfolded and with silent wings,
In unimpassioned mystery the day
  Passes; a lonely thrush its requiem sings.

The dust of night is tangled in the boughs
  Of leafless lime and lilac, and the pine
Grows blacker, and the star upon the brows
  Of sleep is set in heaven for a sign.

Earth's little weary peoples fall on peace
  And dream of breaking buds and blossoming,
Of primrose airs, of days of large increase,
  And all the coloured retinue of spring.

John Drinkwater (1882–1937)

St Vincent's Day

Remember on St Vincent's Day,
If that the sun his beams display,
Be sure to mark his transient beam,
Which through the casement sheds a gleam;
For 'tis a token bright and clear
Of prosperous weather all the year.

Anon

A Frosty Day

Grass afield wears silver thatch;
  Palings all are edged with rime;
Frost-flowers pattern round the latch;
  Cloud nor breeze dissolve the clime;

When the waves are solid floor,
  And the clods are iron-bound,
And the boughs are crystall'd hoar,
  And the red leaf nailed a-ground.

When the fieldfare's flight is slow,
  And a rosy vapour rim,
Now the sun is small and low,
  Belts along the region dim.

When the ice-crack flies and flaws,
  Shore to shore, with thunder shock,
Deeper than the evening daws,
  Clearer than the village clock.

When the rusty blackbird strips,
  Bunch by bunch, the coral thorn;
And the pale day-crescent dips,
  Now to heaven, a slender horn.

Lord de Tabley (1835–1895)

Winter Trees

See the bare arms of the trees!
Ah, it is good that it is winter,
and all the fuss and struggle of leaves is over,
and we may step into the anonymity of winter.

It is good that it is winter,
and the trees are stripped of all the nonsense of leaves,
as one who has shed the pretentions of clothes
is bare unto the soul.

David Austin (1926–2018)

Sheep in Winter

The sheep get up and make their many tracks
And bear a load of snow upon their backs
And gnaw the frozen turnip to the ground
With sharp quick bite and then go noising round
The boy that pecks the turnips all the day
And knocks his hands to keep the cold away
And laps his legs in straw to keep them warm
And hides behind the hedges from the storm
The sheep as tame as dogs go where he goes
And try to shake their fleeces from the snows
Then leave their frozen meal and wander round
The stubble stack that stands beside the ground
And lye all night and face the drizzling storm
And shun the hovel where they might be warm

John Clare (1793–1864)

January

FROM *THE EARTHLY PARADISE*

From this dull rainy undersky and low,
This murky ending of a leaden day,
That never knew the sun, this half-thawed snow,
These tossing black boughs faint against the grey
Of gathering night, thou turnest, dear, away
Silent, but with thy scarce-seen kindly smile
Sent through the dusk my longing to beguile.

There, the lights gleam, and all is dark without!
And in the sudden change our eyes meet dazed –
O look, love, look again! the veil of doubt
Just for one flash, past counting, then was raised!
O eyes of heaven, as clear thy sweet soul blazed
On mine a moment! O come back again
Strange rest and dear amid the long dull pain!

Nay, nay, gone by! though there she sitteth still,
With wide grey eyes so frank and fathomless –
Be patient, heart, thy days they yet shall fill
With utter rest – Yea, now thy pain they bless,
And feed thy last hope of the world's redress –
O unseen hurrying rack! O wailing wind!
What rest and where go ye this night to find?

William Morris (1834–1896)

Wind at Midnight

Naked night; black elms, pallid and streaming sky!
Alone with the passion of the Wind,
In a hollow of stormy sound lost and alone am I,
On beaten earth a lost, unmated mind,
Marvelling at the stars, few, strange, and bright,
That all this dark assault of surging air,
Wrenching the rooted wood, hunting the cloud of night,
As if it would tear all and nothing spare,
Leaves supreme in the height.

Against what laws, what laws, what powers invisible,
Unsought yet always found,
Cries this dumb passion, strains this wrestle of wild will,
With tiger-leaps that seem to shake the ground?
Is it the baffled, homeless, rebel wind's crying
Or storm from a profounder passion wrung?
Ah, heart of man, is it you, the old powers defying,
By far desires and terrible beauty stung,
Broken on laws unseen, in a starry world dying
Ignorant, tameless, young?

Laurence Binyon (1869–1943)

Seasons and Times

VERSES 1–5

Awhile in the dead of the winter,
The wind hurries keen through the sunshine,
But finds no more leaves that may linger
On tree-boughs to strew on the ground.

Long streaks of bright snow-drift, bank-shaded,
Yet lie on the slopes, under hedges;
But still all the road out to Thorndon
Would not wet a shoe on the ground.

The days, though the cold seems to strengthen,
Outlengthen their span, and the evening
Seeks later and later its westing,
To cast its dim hue on the ground,

Till tree-heads shall thicken their shadow
With leaves of a glittering greenness,
And daisies shall fold up their blossoms
At evening, in dew on the ground;

And then, in the plum-warding garden,
Or shadowy orchard, the house-man
Shall smile at his fruit, really blushing,
Where sunheat shoots through on the ground.

William Barnes (1801–1886)

Snowdrop

A pale and pining girl, head bowed, heart gnawed,
whose figure nods and shivers in a shawl
of fine white wool, has suddenly appeared
in the damp woods, as mild and mute as snowfall.
She may not last. She has no strength at all,
but stoops and shakes as if she'd stood all night
on one bare foot, confiding with the moonlight.

One among several hundred clear-eyed ghosts
who get up in the cold and blink and turn
into those trembling emblems of night frosts,
she brings her burnt heart with her in an urn
of ashes, which she opens to re-mourn,
having no other outlet to express
her wild-flower sense of wounded gentleness.

Yes, she's no more now than a drop of snow
on a green stem – her name is now her calling.
Her mind is just a frozen melting glow
of water swollen to the point of falling
which maybe has no meaning. There's no telling.
But what's a beauty, what a mighty power
of patience kept intact is now in flower.

Alice Oswald (1966–)

The Oak

VERSES 1 AND 2

What gnarlèd stretch, what depth of shade, is his!
  There needs no crown to mark the forest's king;
How in his leaves outshines full summer's bliss!
  Sun, storm, rain, dew, to him their tribute bring,
Which he with such benignant royalty
  Accepts, as overpayeth what is lent;
All nature seems his vassal proud to be,
  And cunning only for his ornament.

How towers he, too, amid the billowed snows,
  An unquelled exile from the summer's throne,
Whose plain, uncinctured front more kingly shows,
  Now that the obscuring courtier leaves are flown.
His boughs make music of the winter air,
  Jewelled with sleet, like some cathedral front
Where clinging snow-flakes with quaint art repair
  The dints and furrows of time's envious brunt.

James Russell Lowell (1819–1891)

The Song of the Beasts

(SUNG, ON ONE NIGHT, IN THE CITIES, IN THE DARKNESS)

Come away! Come away!
Ye are sober and dull through the common day,
But now it is night!
It is shameful night, and God is asleep!
(Have you not felt the quick fires that creep
Through the hungry flesh, and the lust of delight,
And hot secrets of dreams that day cannot say?) ...
The house is dumb;
The night calls out to you. – Come, ah, come!
Down the dim stairs, through the creaking door,
Naked, crawling on hands and feet
– It is meet! it is meet!
Ye are men no longer, but less and more,
Beast and God ... Down the lampless street,
By little black ways, and secret places,
In the darkness and mire,
Faint laughter around, and evil faces
By the star-glint seen – ah! follow with us!
For the darkness whispers a blind desire,
And the fingers of night are amorous ...
Keep close as we speed,
Though mad whispers woo you, and hot hands cling,
And the touch and the smell of bare flesh sting,
Soft flank by your flank, and side brushing side –

Tonight never heed!
Unswerving and silent follow with me,
Till the city ends sheer,
And the crook'd lanes open wide,
Out of the voices of night,
Beyond lust and fear,
To the level waters of moonlight,
To the level waters, quiet and clear,
To the black unresting plains of the calling sea.

Rupert Brooke (1887–1915)

FEBRUARY

Wild Skies and Flurrying Snows

Midnight

There are sea and sky about me,
  And yet nothing sense can mark;
For a mist fills all the midnight
  Adding blindness to the dark.

There is not the faintest echo
  From the life of yesterday:
  Not the vaguest stir foretelling
Of a morrow on the way.

'Tis negation's hour of triumph
  In the absence of the sun;
'Tis the hour of endings, ended,
  Of beginnings, unbegun.

Yet the voice of awful silence
  Bids my waiting spirit hark;
There is action in the stillness,
  There is progress in the dark.

In the drift of things and forces
  Comes the better from the worse;
Swings the whole of Nature upward,
  Wakes, and thinks – a universe.

There will be more life tomorrow,
  And of life, more life that knows;
Though the sum of force be constant
  Yet the Living ever grows.

So we sing of evolution,
  And step strongly on our ways;
And we live through nights in patience
  And we learn the worth of days.

Louisa Bevington (1845–1895)

The Thrush in February

VERSES 1–5

I know him, February's thrush,
And loud at eve he valentines
On sprays that paw the naked bush
Where soon will sprout the thorns and bines.

Now ere the foreign singer thrills
Our vale his plain-song pipe he pours,
A herald of the million bills;
And heed him not, the loss is yours.

My study, flanked with ivied fir
And budded beech with dry leaves curled,
Perched over yew and juniper,
He neighbours, piping to his world: –

The wooded pathways dank on brown,
The branches on grey cloud a web,
The long green roller of the down,
An image of the deluge-ebb: –

And farther, they may hear along
The stream beneath the poplar row.
By fits, like welling rocks, the song
Spouts of a blushful Spring in flow.

George Meredith (1828–1909)

Moon of Half-candied Meres

PRAELUDIUM, II

Moon of half-candied meres
And flurrying, fading snows;
Moon of unkindly rains,
Wild skies, and troubled vanes;
When the Norther snarls and bites,
And the lone moon walks a-cold,
And the lawns grizzle o' nights,
And wet fogs search the fold:
Here in this heart of mine
A dream that warms like wine,
A dream one other knows,
Moon of the roaring weirs
And the sip-sopping close,
  February Fill-Dyke,
Shapes like a royal rose –
  A red, red rose!

O, but the distance clears!
O, but the daylight grows!
Soon shall the pied wind-flowers
Babble of greening hours,
Primrose and daffodil
Yearn to a fathering sun,
The lark have all his will,
The thrush be never done,
And April, May, and June
Go to the same blythe tune
As this blythe dream of mine!
Moon when the crocus peers,
Moon when the violet blows,
  February Fair-Maid,
Haste, and let come the rose –
  Let come the rose!

W. E. Henley (1849–1903)

The Tide Rises, the Tide Falls

The tide rises, the tide falls,
The twilight darkens, the curlew calls;
Along the sea-sands damp and brown
The traveller hastens toward the town,
   And the tide rises, the tide falls.

Darkness settles on roofs and walls,
But the sea, the sea in the darkness calls;
The little waves, with their soft, white hands,
Efface the footprints in the sands,
   And the tide rises, the tide falls.

The morning breaks; the steeds in their stalls
Stamp and neigh, as the hostler calls;
The day returns, but nevermore
Returns the traveller to the shore,
   And the tide rises, the tide falls.

Henry Wadsworth Longfellow (1807–1882)

A Winter Piece

LINES 57–70

But winter has yet brighter scenes, – he boasts
Splendours beyond what gorgeous summer knows;
Or autumn with his many fruits, and woods
All flushed with many hues. Come, when the rains
Have glazed the snow, and clothed the trees with ice;
While the slant sun of February pours
Into the bowers a flood of light. Approach!
The encrusted surface shall upbear thy steps,
And the broad arching portals of the grove
Welcome thy entering. Look! the massy trunks
Are cased in the pure chrystal, each light spray,
Nodding and tinkling in the breath of heaven,
Is studded with its trembling water-drops,
That stream with rainbow radiance as they move.

William Cullen Bryant (1794–1878)

Chamber Music XXXV

All day I hear the noise of waters
  Making moan,
Sad as the sea-bird is when, going
  Forth alone,
He hears the winds cry to the waters'
  Monotone.

The grey winds, the cold winds are blowing
  Where I go.
I hear the noise of many waters
  Far below.
All day, all night, I hear them flowing
  To and fro.

James Joyce (1882–1941)

Sonnet: To Tartar, a Terrier Beauty

Snowdrop of dogs, with ear of brownest dye,
Like the last orphan leaf of naked tree
Which shudders in black autumn; though by thee,
Of hearing careless and untutored eye,
Not understood articulate speech of men
Nor marked the artificial mind of books,
– The mortal's voice eternized by the pen, –
Yet hast thou thought and language all unknown
To Babel's scholars; oft intensest looks,
Long scrutiny over some dark-veined stone
Dost thou bestow, learning dead mysteries
Of the world's birth-day, oft in eager tone
With quick-tailed fellows bandiest prompt replies,
Solicitudes canine, four-footed amities.

Thomas Lovell Beddoes (1803–1849)

The Blue Bell is the Sweetest Flower

VERSES 1–9

The blue bell is the sweetest flower
That waves in summer air:
Its blossoms have the mightiest power
To soothe my spirit's care.

There is a spell in purple heath
Too wildly, sadly dear;
The violet has a fragrant breath
But fragrance will not cheer.

The trees are bare, the sun is cold,
And seldom, seldom seen;
The heavens have lost their zone of gold
The earth its robe of green.

And ice upon the glancing stream
Has cast its sombre shade
And distant hills and valleys seem
In frozen mist arrayed.

The blue bell cannot charm me now,
The heath has lost its bloom,
The violets in the glen below
They yield no sweet perfume

But though I mourn the heather-bell
'Tis better far, away;
I know how fast my tears would swell
To see it smile today.

And that wood flower that hides so shy
Beneath the mossy stone
Its balmy scent and dewy eye:
'Tis not for them I moan.

It is the slight and stately stem,
The blossom's silvery blue,
The buds hid like a sapphire gem
In sheaths of emerald hue.

'Tis these that breathe upon my heart
A calm and softening spell
That if it makes the tear-drop start
Has power to soothe as well.

Emily Brontë (1818–1848)

9 FEBRUARY

The Gloom that Winter Casts

The gloom that winter casts
  How soon the heart forgets –
When summer brings at last –
  The sun that never sets.
So love – when hope first gleams
  Forgets its former pain –
Amidst those sunny beams
  Which ne'er shall set again.

Edward Lear (1812–1888)

What Makes Summer?

LINES 1–24

Winter froze both brook and well;
Fast and fast the snowflakes fell;
Children gathered round the hearth
Made a summer of their mirth;
When a boy, so lately come
That his life was yet one sum
Of delights – of aimless rambles,
Romps and dreams and games and gambols,
Thought aloud: 'I wish I knew
What makes summer – that I do!'
Father heard, and it did show him
How to write a little poem.

What makes summer, little one,
Do you ask? It is the sun.
Want of heat is all the harm,
Summer is but winter warm.
'Tis the sun – yes, that one there,
Dim and gray, low in the air!
Now he looks at us askance,
But will lift his countenance
Higher up, and look down straighter.
Rise much earlier, set much later,
Till we sing out, 'Hail, Well-comer,
Thou hast brought our own old Summer!'

George MacDonald (1824–1905)

February Twilight

I stood beside a hill
  Smooth with new-laid snow,
A single star looked out
  From the cold evening glow.

There was no other creature
  That saw what I could see –
I stood and watched the evening star
  As long as it watched me.

Sara Teasdale (1884–1933)

A Robin

Ghost-grey the fall of night,
  Ice-bound the lane,
Lone in the dying light
  Flits he again;
Lurking where shadows steal,
Perched in his coat of blood,
Man's homestead at his heel,
  Death-still the wood.

Odd restless child; it's dark;
  All wings are flown
But this one wizard's – hark!
  Stone clapped on stone!
Changeling and solitary,
Secret and sharp and small,
Flits he from tree to tree,
  Calling on all.

Walter de la Mare (1873–1956)

Sonnet

Bright star, would I were steadfast as thou art –
  Not in lone splendour hung aloft the night
And watching, with eternal lids apart,
  Like nature's patient, sleepless Eremite,
The moving waters at their priestlike task
  Of pure ablution round earth's human shores,
Or gazing on the new soft-fallen mask
  Of snow upon the mountains and the moors –
No – yet still steadfast, still unchangeable,
  Pillowed upon my fair love's ripening breast,
To feel for ever its soft fall and swell,
  Awake for ever in a sweet unrest,
Still, still to hear her tender-taken breath,
  And so live ever – or else swoon to death.

John Keats (1795–1821)

Call for the Robin Redbreast and the Wren

Call for the robin-redbreast and the wren,
Since o'er shady groves they hover,
And with leaves and flowers do cover
The friendless bodies of unburied men.
Call unto his funeral dole
The ant, the field-mouse, and the mole,
To rear him hillocks that shall keep him warm
And, when gay tombs are robbed, sustain no harm;
But keep the wolf far thence, that's foe to men,
For with his nails he'll dig them up again.

John Webster (c.1580–c.1625)

The Mountain

The burn ran blacker for the snow
And ice-floe on ice-floe
Jangled in heavy lurches
Beneath the claret-coloured birches.

Dark grouse rose becking from the ground
And deer turned sharp heads round,
The antlers on their brows
Like stunted trees with withered boughs.

I climbed to where the mountain sloped
And long wan bubbles groped
Under the ice's cover,
A bridge that groaned as I crossed over.

I reached the mist, brighter than day,
That showed a specious way
By narrow crumbling shelves,
Where rocks grew larger than themselves.

But when I saw the mountain's spire
Looming through that damp fire,
I left it unwon
And climbed down to the setting sun.

Andrew Young (1885–1971)

Hope

O thrush, is it true?
  Your song tells
Of a world born anew,
Of fields gold with buttercups, woodlands all blue
  With hyacinth bells;
Of primroses deep
  In the moss of the lane,
Of a Princess asleep
And dear magic to do.
Will the sun wake the princess? O thrush, is it true?
  Will Spring come again?

Will Spring come again?
  Now at last
With soft shine and rain
Will the violet be sweet where the dead leaves have lain?
  Will Winter be past?
In the brown of the copse
  Will white wind-flowers star through
Where the last oak-leaf drops?
  Will the daisies come too,
And the may and the lilac? Will Spring come again?
  O thrush, is it true?

E. Nesbit (1858–1924)

Water-Fowl

OBSERVED FREQUENTLY OVER THE LAKES
OF RYDAL AND GRASMERE

Mark how the feathered tenants of the flood,
With grace of motion that might scarcely seem
Inferior to angelical, prolong
Their curious pastime! shaping in mid air
(And sometimes with ambitious wing that soars
High as the level of the mountain-tops)
A circuit ampler than the lake beneath –
Their own domain; but ever, while intent
On tracing and retracing that large round,
Their jubilant activity evolves
Hundreds of curves and circlets, to and fro,
Upward and downward, progress intricate
Yet unperplexed, as if one spirit swayed
Their indefatigable flight. 'Tis done –
Ten times, or more, I fancied it had ceased;
But lo! the vanished company again
Ascending; they approach – I hear their wings,
Faint, faint at first; and then an eager sound,
Past in a moment – and as faint again!
They tempt the sun to sport amid their plumes;
They tempt the water, or the gleaming ice,
To show them a fair image; 'tis themselves,
Their own fair forms, upon the glimmering plain,
Painted more soft and fair as they descend
Almost to touch; – then up again aloft,
Up with a sally and a flash of speed,
As if they scorned both resting-place and rest!

William Wordsworth (1770–1850)

In Dark Weather

Against the gaunt, brown-purple hill
The bright brown oak is brown and bare;
A pale-brown flock is feeding there –
    Contented, still.

No bracken lights the bleak hill-side;
No leaves are on the branches wide;
No lambs across the fields have cried;
    – Not yet.

But whorl by whorl the green fronds climb;
The ewes are patient till their time;
The warm buds swell beneath the rime –
    For life does not forget.

Mary Webb (1881–1927)

West Wind in Winter

Another day awakes. And who –
  Changing the world – is this?
He comes at whiles, the winter through,
  West Wind! I would not miss
His sudden tryst: the long, the new
  Surprises of his kiss.

Vigilant, I make haste to close
  With him who comes my way.
I go to meet him as he goes;
  I know his note, his lay,
His colour and his morning-rose,
  And I confess his day.

My window waits; at dawn I hark
  His call; at morn I meet
His haste around the tossing park
  And down the softened street;
The gentler light is his; the dark.
  The grey – he turns it sweet.

So too, so too, do I confess
  My poet when he sings.
He rushes on my mortal guess
  With his immortal things.
I feel, I know him. On I press –
  He finds me 'twixt his wings.

Alice Meynell (1847–1922)

20 FEBRUARY

February

FROM *THE EARTHLY PARADISE*

The change has come at last, and from the west
Drives on the wind, and gives the clouds no rest,
And ruffles up the water thin that lies
Over the surface of the thawing ice;
Sunrise and sunset with no glorious show
Are seen, as late they were across the snow;
The wet-lipped west wind chilleth to the bone
More than the light and flickering east hath done.
Full soberly the earth's fresh hope begins,
Nor stays to think of what each new day wins:
And still it seems to bid us turn away
From this chill thaw to dream of blossomed May:

William Morris (1834–1896)

To Jane: The Invitation

LINES 1–46

Best and brightest, come away!
Fairer far than this fair Day,
Which, like thee to those in sorrow,
Comes to bid a sweet good-morrow
To the rough Year just awake
In its cradle on the brake
The brightest hour of unborn Spring,
Through the winter wandering,
Found, it seems, the halcyon Morn
To hoar February born.
Bending from Heaven, in azure mirth,
It kiss'd the forehead of the Earth,
And smiled upon the silent sea,
And bade the frozen streams be free,
And waked to music all their fountains,
And breathed upon the frozen mountains,
And like a prophetess of May
Strewed flowers upon the barren way,
Making the wintry world appear
Like one on whom thou smilest, dear
Away, away, from men and towns,
To the wild wood and the downs –
To the silent wilderness
Where the soul need not repress
Its music lest it should not find
An echo in another's mind,

While the touch of Nature's art
Harmonizes heart to heart.
I leave this notice on my door
For each accustomed visitor: –
'I am gone into the fields
To take what this sweet hour yields; –
Reflection, you may come to-morrow,
Sit by the fireside with Sorrow. –
You with the unpaid bill, Despair, –
You, tiresome verse-reciter, Care, –
I will pay you in the grave, –
Death will listen to your stave.
Expectation too, be off!
To-day is for itself enough;
Hope, in pity mock not Woe
With smiles, nor follow where I go;
Long having lived on thy sweet food,
At length I find one moment's good
After long pain – with all your love,
That you never told me of.'

Percy Bysshe Shelley (1792–1822)

The Secret

In the profoundest ocean
There is a rainbow shell,
It is always there, shining most stilly
Under the greatest storm waves
And under the happy little waves
That the old Greek called 'ripples of laughter'
And you listen, the rainbow shell
Sings – in the profoundest ocean.
It is always there, singing most silently!

Katherine Mansfield (1888–1923)

The Robin

The Robin is a Gabriel
In humble circumstances –
His Dress denotes him socially,
Of Transport's Working Classes –
He has the punctuality
Of the New England Farmer –
The same oblique integrity,
A Vista vastly warmer –

A small but sturdy Residence
A self denying Household,
The Guests of Perspicacity
Are all that cross his Threshold –
As covert as a Fugitive,
Cajoling Consternation
By Ditties to the Enemy
And Sylvan Punctuation –

Emily Dickinson (1830–1886)

Winter Heavens

Sharp is the night, but stars with frost alive
Leap off the rim of earth across the dome.
It is a night to make the heavens our home
More than the nest whereto apace we strive.
Lengths down our road each fir-tree seems a hive,
In swarms outrushing from the golden comb.
They waken waves of thoughts that burst to foam:
The living throb in me, the dead revive.
Yon mantle clothes us: there, past mortal breath,
Life glistens on the river of the death.
It folds us, flesh and dust; and have we knelt,
Or never knelt, or eyed as kine the springs
Of radiance, the radiance enrings:
And this is the soul's haven to have felt.

George Meredith (1828–1909)

Craving for Spring

LINES 1–12

I wish it were spring in the world.

Let it be spring!
Come, bubbling, surging tide of sap!
Come, rush of creation!
Come, life! surge through this mass of mortification!
Come, sweep away these exquisite, ghastly first-flowers,
which are rather last-flowers!
Come, thaw down their cool portentousness, dissolve them:
snowdrops, straight, death-veined exhalations of white and
 purple crocuses,
flowers of the penumbra, issue of corruption, nourished in
 mortification,
jets of exquisite finality;
Come, spring, make havoc of them!

D. H. Lawrence (1885–1930)

26 FEBRUARY

Thaw

Over the land freckled with snow half-thawed
The speculating rooks at their nests cawed
And saw from elm-tops, delicate as flower of grass,
What we below could not see, Winter pass.

Edward Thomas (1878–1917)

Look Through the Naked Bramble and Black Thorn

Look through the naked bramble and black thorn
And see the arum show its vivid green
Glossy and rich and some ink spotted like the morn
Ing sky with clouds – in sweetest neuks I've been
And seen the arum sprout its happy green
Full of spring visions and green thoughts o' may
Dead leaves a' litter where its leaves are seen
Broader and brighter green from day to day
Beneath the hedges in their leafless spray

John Clare (1793–1864)

The Door of Spring

How shall we open the door of Spring
  That Winter is holding wearily shut?
    Though winds are calling and waters brawling,
    And snow decaying and light delaying,
  Yet will it not move in its yielding rut
And back on its flowery hinges swing,
      Till wings are flapping
      And woodpeckers tapping
      With sharp, clear rapping
        At the door of Spring.

How shall we fasten the door of Spring
  Wide, so wide that it cannot close?
    Though buds are filling and frogs are trilling,
    And violets breaking and grass awaking,
  Yet doubtfully back and forth it blows
Till come the birds, and the woodlands ring
      With sharp beak stammer –
      The sudden clamor
      Of the woodpecker's hammer
        At the door of Spring.

Ethelwyn Wetherald (1857–1940)

Winter's Turning

Snow is still on the ground,
But there is a golden brightness in the air.
Across the river,
Blue,
Blue,
Sweeping widely under the arches
Of many bridges,
Is a spire and a dome,
Clear as though ringed with ice-flakes,
Golden, and pink, and jocund.
On a near-by steeple,
A golden weather-cock flashes smartly,
His open beak 'Cock-a-doodle-dooing'
Straight at the ear of Heaven.
A tall apartment house,
Crocus-coloured,
Thrusts up from the street
Like a new-sprung flower.
Another street is edged and patterned
With the bloom of bricks,
Houses and houses of rose-red bricks,
Every window a-glitter.
The city is a parterre,
Blowing and glowing,
Alight with the wind,
Washed over with gold and mercury.

Let us throw up our hats,
For we are past the age of balls
And have none handy.
Let us take hold of hands,
And race along the sidewalks,
And dodge the traffic in crowded streets.
Let us whir with the golden spoke-wheels
Of the sun.
For to-morrow Winter drops into the waste-basket,
And the calendar calls it March.

Amy Lowell (1874–1925)

MARCH

Green Leaves and Blossoms

March, You Old Blusterer

March, you old blusterer,
  What will you bring?
Sunny days, stormy days,
  Under your wing?
No matter which it be,
  You will bring spring.

Whether Lion roaring comes
  Over bleak hills,
Whether Lamb bleating goes
  Seeking sweet rills,
You will bring primroses
  And daffodils.

Whether the earth shows a
  White or green quilt,
Where in both hedge and tree
  Men hear a lilt,
March, you old blusterer
  Nests will be built.

Eleanor Farjeon (1881–1965)

To Primroses Fill'd with Morning-dew

Why doe ye weep, sweet Babes? can Tears
Speak griefe in you,
Who were but borne
Just as the modest Morne
Teem'd her refreshing dew?
Alas you have not known that shower,
That marres a flower;
Nor felt th'unkind
Breath of a blasting wind;
Nor are ye worne with yeares;
Or warpt, as we,
Who think it strange to see,
Such pretty flowers, (like to Orphans young)
To speak by Teares, before ye have a Tongue.

Speak, whimp'ring Younglings, and make known
The reason, why
Ye droop, and weep;
Is it for want of sleep?
Or childish Lullabie?
Or that ye have not seen as yet
The *Violet*?
Or brought a kisse
From that Sweet-heart to this?
No, no, this sorrow shown
By your teares shed
Wo'd have this Lecture read,
That things of greatest, so of meanest worth,
Conceiv'd with grief are, and with teares brought forth.

Robert Herrick (1591–1674)

It Came with the Year's First Crocus

PRAELUDIUM, IV

It came with the year's first crocus
  In a world of winds and snows –
Because it would, because it must,
Because of life and time and lust;
And a year's first crocus served my turn
  As well as the year's first rose.

The March rack hurries and hectors,
  The March dust heaps and blows;
But the primrose flouts the daffodil,
And here's the patient violet still;
And the year's first crocus brought me luck,
  So hey for the year's first rose!

W. E. Henley (1849–1903)

4 MARCH

Early Spring

VERSES I–V

I

Once more the Heavenly Power
  Makes all things new,
And domes the red-plow'd hills
  With loving blue;
The blackbirds have their wills,
  The throstles too.

II

Opens a door in Heaven;
  From skies of glass
A Jacob's ladder falls
  On greening grass,
And o'er the mountain-walls
  Young angels pass.

III

Before them fleets the shower,
  And burst the buds,
And shine the level lands,
  And flash the floods;
The stars are from their hands
  Flung thro' the woods,

IV

The woods with living airs
  How softly fann'd,
Light airs from where the deep,
  All down the sand,
Is breathing in his sleep,
  Heard by the land.

V

O follow, leaping blood,
  The season's lure!
O heart, look down and up
  Serene, secure,
Warm as the crocus cup,
  Like snow-drops, pure!

Alfred, Lord Tennyson (1809–1892)

A Thrush in the Trenches

FROM *THE SOLDIER*

Suddenly he sang across the trenches,
   vivid in the fleeting hush
as a star-shell through the smashed black branches,
   a more than English thrush.

Suddenly he sang, and those who listened
   nor moved nor wondered, but
heard, all bewitched, the sweet unhastened
   crystal Magnificat.

One crouched, a muddied rifle clasping,
   and one a filled grenade,
but little cared they, while he went lisping
   the one clear tune he had.

Paused horror, hate and Hell a moment,
   (you could almost hear the sigh)
and still he sang to them, and so went
   (suddenly) singing by.

Humbert Wolfe (1885–1940)

Spring Night

Through the smothered air the wicker finds
A muttering voice, 'crick' cries the embered ash.
Sharp rains knap at the panes beyond the blinds,
The flues and eaves moan, the jarred windows clash;
And like a sea breaking its barriers, flooding
New green abysses with untold uproar.
The cataract nightwind whelms the time of budding.
Swooping in sightless fury off the moor
Into our valley. Not a star shines. Who
Would guess the martin and the cuckoo come,
The pear in bloom, the bloom gone from the plum.
The cowslips countless as a morning dew?
So mad it blows, so truceless and so grim.
As if day's host of flowers were a moment's whim.

Edmund Blunden (1896–1974)

Answer to a Child's Question

Do you ask what the birds say? The Sparrow, the Dove,
The Linnet and Thrush say, 'I love and I love!'
In the winter they're silent – the wind is so strong;
What it says, I don't know, but it sings a loud song.
But green leaves, and blossoms, and sunny warm weather,
And singing, and loving – all come back together.
But the Lark is so brimful of gladness and love,
The green fields below him, the blue sky above,
That he sings, and he sings; and forever sings he –
'I love my Love, and my Love loves me!'

Samuel Taylor Coleridge (1772–1834)

Very Early Spring

The fields are snowbound no longer;
There are little blue lakes and flags of tenderest green.
The snow has been caught up into the sky –
So many white clouds – and the blue of the sky is cold.
Now the sun walks in the forest,
He touches the bows and stems with his golden fingers;
They shiver, and wake from slumber.
Over the barren branches he shakes his yellow curls.
. . . Yet is the forest full of the sound of tears . . .
A wind dances over the fields.
Shrill and clear the sound of her waking laughter,
Yet the little blue lakes tremble
And the flags of tenderest green bend and quiver.

Katherine Mansfield (1888–1923)

9 MARCH

Winter Moon

How thin and sharp is the moon tonight!
How thin and sharp and ghostly white
Is the slim curved crook of the moon tonight!

Langston Hughes (1901–1967)

A Light Exists in Spring

A Light exists in Spring
Not present on the Year
At any other period –
When March is scarcely here

A Color stands abroad
On Solitary Fields
That Science cannot overtake
But Human Nature feels.

It waits upon the Lawn,
It shows the furthest Tree
Upon the furthest Slope you know
It almost speaks to you.

Then as Horizons step
Or Noons report away
Without the Formula of sound
It passes and we stay –

A quality of loss
Affecting our Content
As Trade had suddenly encroached
Upon a Sacrament.

Emily Dickinson (1830–1886)

A Forest Lake

O lake of sylvan shore! when gentle Spring
Slopes down upon thee from the mountain side,
When birds begin to build and brood and sing;
Or, in maturer season, when the pied
And fragrant turf is throng'd with blossoms rare;
In the frore sweetness of the breathing morn,
When the loud echoes of the herdsman's horn
Do sally forth upon the silent air
Of thy thick forestry, may I be there,
While the wood waits to see its phantom born
At clearing twilight, in thy grassy breast;
Or, when cool eve is busy, on thy shores,
With trails of purple shadow from the West,
Or dusking in the wake of tardy oars.

Charles Tennyson Turner (1808–1879)

Green

The dawn was apple-green,
  The sky was green wine held up in the sun,
The moon was a golden petal between.

She opened her eyes, and green
  They shone, clear like flowers undone
For the first time, now for the first time seen.

D. H. Lawrence (1885–1930)

There was an Old Man in a Tree

There was an Old Man in a tree,
Whose whiskers were lovely to see;
But the birds of the air pluck'd them perfectly bare,
To make themselves nests in that tree.

Edward Lear (1812–1888)

The Soul of Love

FROM *SPRING, THE SEASONS*

When first the soul of love is sent abroad,
Warm through the vital air, and on the heart
Harmonious seizes, the gay troops begin,
In gallant thought, to plume the painted wing,
And try again the long-forgotten strain;
At first faint-warbled: but no sooner grows
The soft infusion prevalent, and wide,
Than, all alive, at once their joy o'erflows
In music unconfined. Up springs the lark,
Shrill-voiced, and loud, the messenger of morn;
Ere yet the shadows fly, he mounted sings
Amid the dawning clouds, and from their haunts
Calls up the tuneful nations. Every copse
Deep-tangled, tree irregular, and bush
Bending with dewy moisture, o'er the heads

Of the coy choristers that lodge within,
Are prodigal of harmony. The thrush
And wood-lark, o'er the kind contending throng
Superior heard, run through the sweetest length
Of notes; when listening Philomela deigns
To let them joy, and purposes, in thought
Elate, to make her night excel their day.

James Thomson (1700–1748)

Soil

On this day, the breathing earth
gave this little primrose birth.
On this day the living soil
yielded up its golden spoil.
Engaged in such a noble toil,
who despises simple soil?

David Austin (1926–2018)

The Dalliance of the Eagles

Skirting the river road, (my forenoon walk, my rest,)
Skyward in air a sudden muffled sound, the dalliance of the eagles,
The rushing amorous contact high in space together,
The clinching interlocking claws, a living, fierce, gyrating wheel,
Four beating wings, two beaks, a swirling mass tight grappling,
In tumbling turning clustering loops, straight downward falling,
Till o'er the river pois'd, the twain yet one, a moment's lull,
A motionless still balance in the air, then parting, talons loosing,
Upward again on slow-firm pinions slanting, their separate diverse flight,
She hers, he his, pursuing.

Walt Whitman (1819–1892)

17 MARCH

But These Things Also

But these things also are Spring's –
On banks by the roadside the grass
Long-dead that is greyer now
Than all the Winter it was;

The shell of a little snail bleached
In the grass; chip of flint, and mite
Of chalk; and the small birds' dung
In splashes of purest white:

All the white things a man mistakes
For earliest violets
Who seeks through Winter's ruins
Something to pay Winter's debts,

While the North blows, and starling flocks
By chattering on and on
Keep their spirits up in the mist,
And Spring's here, Winter's not gone.

Edward Thomas (1878–1917)

Four Ducks on a Pond

Four ducks on a pond,
A grass-bank beyond,
A blue sky of spring,
White clouds on the wing;
What a little thing
To remember for years –
To remember with tears!

William Allingham (1824–1889)

There Will Come Soft Rains

(WAR TIME)

There will come soft rains and the smell of the ground,
And swallows circling with their shimmering sound;

And frogs in the pools singing at night,
And wild-plum trees in tremulous white;

Robins will wear their feathery fire,
Whistling their whims on a low fence-wire;

And not one will know of the war, not one
Will care at last when it is done.

Not one would mind, neither bird nor tree,
If mankind perished utterly;

And Spring herself, when she woke at dawn
Would scarcely know that we were gone.

Sara Teasdale (1884–1933)

20 MARCH

The Fish

LINES 1–37

In a cool curving world he lies
And ripples with dark ecstasies.
The kind luxurious lapse and steal
Shapes all his universe to feel
And know and be; the clinging stream
Closes his memory, glooms his dream,
Who lips the roots o' the shore, and glides
Superb on unreturning tides.
Those silent waters weave for him
A fluctuant mutable world and dim,
Where wavering masses bulge and gape
Mysterious, and shape to shape
Dies momently through whorl and hollow,
And form and line and solid follow
Solid and line and form to dream
Fantastic down the eternal stream;
An obscure world, a shifting world,
Bulbous, or pulled to thin, or curled,
Or serpentine, or driving arrows,
Or serene slidings, or March narrows.
There slipping wave and shore are one,
And weed and mud. No ray of sun,
But glow to glow fades down the deep

(As dream to unknown dream in sleep);
Shaken translucency illumes
The hyaline of drifting glooms;
The strange soft-handed depth subdues
Drowned colour there, but black to hues,
As death to living, decomposes –
Red darkness of the heart of roses,
Blue brilliant from dead starless skies,
And gold that lies behind the eyes,
The unknown unnameable sightless white
That is the essential flame of night,
Lustreless purple, hooded green,
The myriad hues that lie between
Darkness and darkness! ...

Rupert Brooke (1887–1915)

I Watched a Blackbird

I watched a blackbird on a budding sycamore
One Easter Day, when sap was stirring twigs to the core;
  I saw his tongue, and crocus-coloured bill
  Parting and closing as he turned his trill;
  Then he flew down, seized on a stem of hay,
And upped to where his building scheme was under way,
As if so sure a nest were never shaped on spray.

Thomas Hardy (1840–1928)

To Violets

Welcome, Maids of Honour,
You doe bring
In the Spring;
And wait upon her.

She has Virgins many,
Fresh and faire;
Yet you are
More sweet than any.

Y'are the Maiden Posies;
And so grac't,
To be plac't,
'Fore Damask Roses.

Yet, though thus respected,
By and by
Ye doe lie,
Poore Girles, neglected.

Robert Herrick (1591–1674)

To a Cat

PART I, VERSES 1–3

Stately, kindly, lordly friend,
   Condescend
Here to sit by me, and turn
Glorious eyes that smile and burn,
Golden eyes, love's lustrous meed,
On the golden page I read.

All your wondrous wealth of hair,
   Dark and fair,
Silken-shaggy, soft and bright
As the clouds and beams of night,
Pays my reverent hand's caress
Back with friendlier gentleness.

Dogs may fawn on all and some
   As they come;
You, a friend of loftier mind,
Answer friends alone in kind.
Just your foot upon my hand
Softly bids it understand.

Algernon Charles Swinburne (1837–1909)

24 MARCH

The Enkindled Spring

This spring as it comes bursts up in bonfires green,
Wild puffing of green-fire trees, and flame-filled bushes,
Thorn-blossom lifting in wreaths of smoke between
Where the wood fumes up and the flickering, watery
  rushes.

I am amazed at this spring, this conflagration
Of green fires lit on the soil of the earth, this blaze
Of growing, these smoke-puffs that puff in wild gyration,
Faces of people blowing across my gaze!

And I, what sort of fire am I among
This conflagration of spring? the gap in it all – !
Not even palish smoke like the rest of the throng.
Less than the wind that runs to the flamy call!

D. H. Lawrence (1885–1930)

The Fields of Flanders

Last year the fields were all glad and gay
With silver daisies and silver may;
There were kingcups gold by the river's edge
And primrose stars under every hedge.

This year the fields are trampled and brown,
The hedges are broken and beaten down,
And where the primroses used to grow
Are little black crosses set in a row.

And the flower of hopes, and the flower of dreams,
The noble, fruitful, beautiful schemes,
The tree of life with its fruit and bud,
Are trampled down in the mud and the blood.

The changing seasons will bring again
The magic of Spring to our wood and plain:
Though the Spring be so green as never was seen
The crosses will still be black in the green.

The God of battles shall judge the foe
Who trampled our country and laid her low ...
God! hold our hands on the reckoning day,
Lest all we owe them we should repay.

E. Nesbit (1858–1924)

The Blackbird

VERSES 1–3

Ov all the birds upon the wing
Between the zunny show'rs o' spring, –
Vor all the lark, a-swingèn high,
Mid zing below a cloudless sky,
An' sparrows, clust'rèn roun' the bough,
Mid chatter to the men at plough, –
The blackbird, whisslèn in among
The boughs, do zing the gaÿest zong.

Vor we do hear the blackbird zing
His sweetest ditties in the spring,
When nippèn win's noo mwore do blow
Vrom northern skies, wi' sleet or snow,
But drēve light doust along between
The leäne-zide hedges, thick an' green;
An' zoo the blackbird in among
The boughs do zing the gaÿest zong.

'Tis blithe, wi' newly-open'd eyes,
To zee the mornèn's ruddy skies;
Or, out a-haulèn frith or lops
Vrom new-plēshed hedge or new-vell'd copse,
To rest at noon in primrwose beds
Below the white-bark'd woak-trees' heads;
But there's noo time, the whole daÿ long,
Lik' evenèn wi' the blackbird's zong.

William Barnes (1801–1886)

27 MARCH

Little Gidding

I, LINES 1–20

Midwinter spring is its own season
Sempiternal though sodden towards sundown,
Suspended in time, between pole and tropic.
When the short day is brightest, with frost and fire,
The brief sun flames the ice, on pond and ditches,
In windless cold that is the heart's heat,
Reflecting in a watery mirror
A glare that is blindness in the early afternoon.
And glow more intense than blaze of branch, or brazier,
Stirs the dumb spirit: no wind, but pentecostal fire
In the dark time of the year. Between melting and freezing
The soul's sap quivers. There is no earth smell
Or smell of living thing. This is the spring time
But not in time's covenant. Now the hedgerow
Is blanched for an hour with transitory blossom
Of snow, a bloom more sudden
Than that of summer, neither budding nor fading,
Not in the scheme of generation.
Where is the summer, the unimaginable
Zero summer?

T. S. Eliot (1888–1965)

Night-piece

Now independent, beautiful and proud,
Out of the vanishing body of a cloud
Like its arisen soul the full moon swims
Over the sea, into whose distant brims
Has flowed the last of the light. I am alone.
Even the diving gannet now is flown
From these unpeopled sands. A mist lies cold
Upon the muffled boundaries of the world.
The lovely earth whose silence is so deep
Is folded up in the night, but not in sleep.

Eleanor Farjeon (1881–1965)

29 MARCH

The Progress of Spring

VERSES I AND II

The groundflame of the crocus breaks the mould,
Fair Spring slides hither o'er the Southern sea,
Wavers on her thin stem the snowdrop cold
That trembles not to kisses of the bee:
Come, Spring, for now from all the dripping eaves
The spear of ice has wept itself away,
And hour by hour unfolding woodbine leaves
O'er his uncertain shadow droops the day.
She comes! The loosen'd rivulets run;
The frost-bead melts upon her golden hair;
Her mantle, slowly greening in the Sun,
Now wraps her close, now arching leaves her bare
To breaths of balmier air.

Up leaps the lark, gone wild to welcome her,
About her glance the tits, and shriek the jays,
Before her skims the jubilant woodpecker,
The linnet's bosom blushes at her gaze,
While round her brows a woodland culver flits,
Watching her large light eyes and gracious looks,
And in her open palm a halcyon sits
Patient – the secret splendour of the brooks.
Come, Spring! She comes on waste and wood,
On farm and field: but enter also here,
Diffuse thyself at will thro' all my blood,
And, tho' thy violet sicken into sere,
Lodge with me all the year!

Alfred, Lord Tennyson (1809–1892)

Stars, I Have Seen them Fall

Stars, I have seen them fall,
  But when they drop and die
No star is lost at all
  From all the star-sown sky.
The toil of all that be
  Helps not the primal fault;
It rains into the sea,
  And still the sea is salt.

A. E. Housman (1859–1936)

The Beech-Tree's Petition

O leave this barren spot to me!
Spare, woodman, spare the beechen tree!
Though bush or floweret never grow
My dark unwarming shade below;
Nor summer bud perfume the dew
Of rosy blush, or yellow hue;
Nor fruits of autumn, blossom-born,
My green and glossy leaves adorn;
Nor murmuring tribes from me derive
The ambrosial amber of the hive;
Yet leave this barren spot to me:
Spare, woodman, spare the beechen tree!

Thrice twenty summers I have seen
The sky grow bright, the forest green;
And many a wintry wind have stood
In bloomless, fruitless solitude,
Since childhood in my pleasant bower
First spent its sweet and sportive hour,
Since youthful lovers in my shade
Their vows of truth and rapture made;
And on my trunk's surviving frame
Carved many a long-forgotten name.
Oh! by the sighs of gentle sound,
First breathed upon this sacred ground;
By all that Love has whispered here,
Or Beauty heard with ravished ear;
As Love's own altar honour me:
Spare, woodman, spare the beechen tree!

Thomas Campbell (1777–1844)

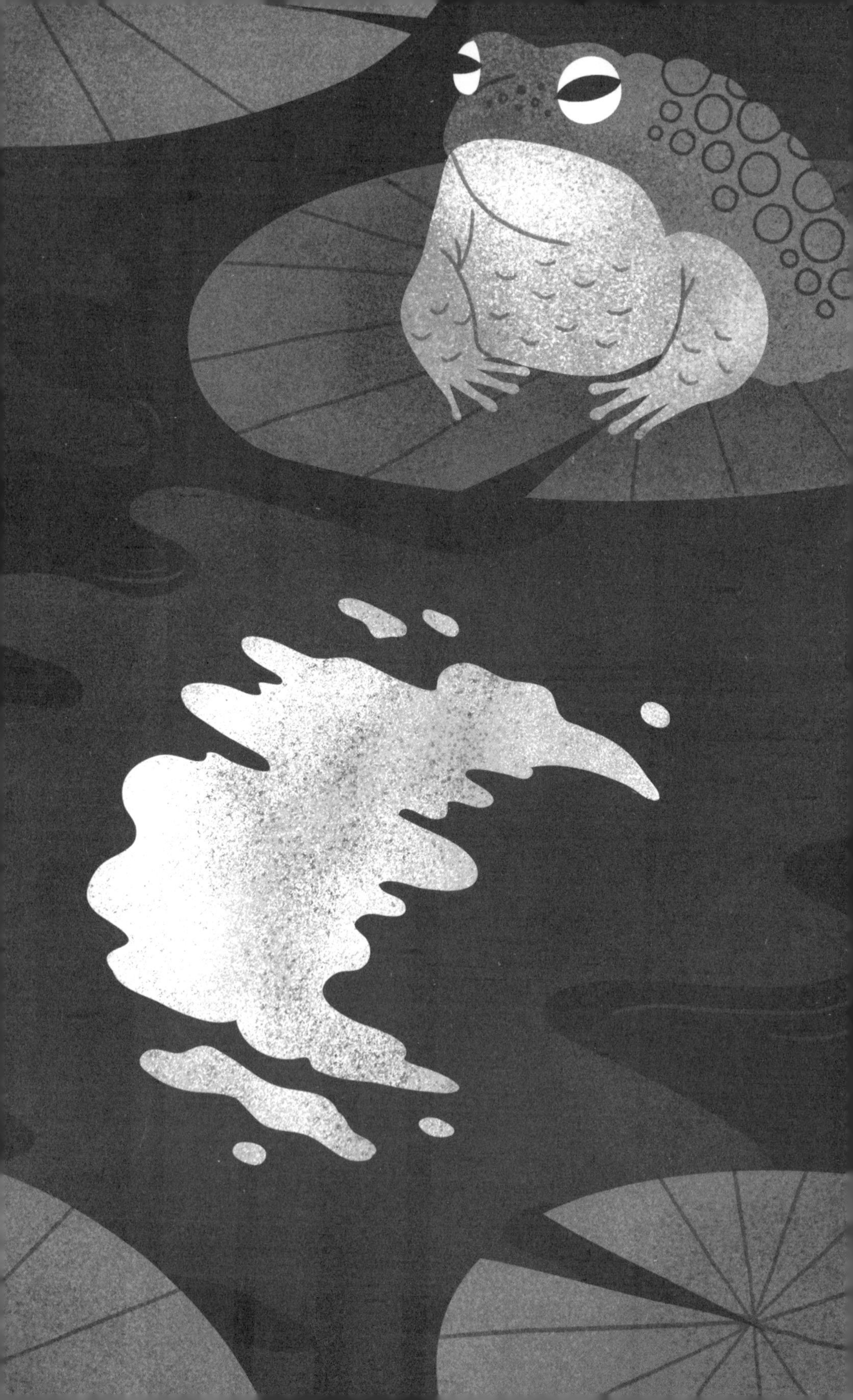

APRIL

The Nightingale Begins its Song

Home Thoughts from Abroad

I

Oh, to be in England
Now that April's there,
And whoever wakes in England
Sees, some morning, unaware,
That the lowest boughs and brushwood sheaf
Round the elm-tree bole are in tiny leaf,
While the chaffinch sings on the orchard bough
In England – now!

II

And after April, when May follows,
And the whitethroat builds, and all the swallows!
Hark, where my blossomed pear-tree in the hedge
Leans to the field and scatters on the clover
Blossoms and dewdrops – at the bent spray's edge –
That's the wise thrush; he sings each song twice over,
Lest you should think he never could recapture
The first fine careless rapture!
And though the fields look rough with hoary dew
All will be gay when noontide wakes anew
The buttercups, the little children's dower
– Far brighter than this gaudy melon-flower!

Robert Browning (1812–1889)

Twelve Songs: V

Dog The single creature leads a partial life,
Man by his mind, and by his nose the hound;
He needs the deep emotions I can give,
I scent him in a vaster hunting ground.

Cats Like calls to like, to share is to relieve
And sympathy the root bears love the flower;
He feels with us, and in him we perceive
A common passion for the lonely hour.

Cats We move in our apartness and our pride
About the decent dwellings he has made:
Dog In all his walks I follow at his side,
His faithful servant and his loving shade.

W. H. Auden (1907–1973)

The Woodspurge

The wind flapped loose, the wind was still,
Shaken out dead from tree and hill:
I had walked on at the wind's will, –
I sat now, for the wind was still.

Between my knees my forehead was, –
My lips, drawn in, said not Alas!
My hair was over in the grass,
My naked ears heard the day pass.

My eyes, wide open, had the run
Of some ten weeds to fix upon;
Among those few, out of the sun,
The woodspurge flowered, three cups in one.

From perfect grief there need not be
Wisdom or even memory:
One thing then learnt remains to me, –
The woodspurge has a cup of three.

D. G. Rossetti (1828–1882)

Scale Force, Cumberland

It sweeps, as sweeps an army
Adown the mountain-side,
With the voice of many thunders
Like the battle's sounding tide.

Yet the sky is blue above it,
And the dashing of the spray
Wears the colour of the rainbow
Upon an April day.

It rejoices in the sunshine
When after heavy rain
It gathers the far waters
To dash upon the plain.

It is terrible yet lovely
Beneath the morning rays,
Like a dream of strength and beauty
It haunted those who gaze.

We feel that it is glorious –
Its power is on the soul –
And lofty thoughts within us
Acknowledge its control.

A generous inspiration
Is on the outward world –
It waketh thoughts and feelings
In a careless coldness furled.

To love and to admire
Seems natural to the heart;
Life's small and selfish interests
From such a scene depart!

Letitia Elizabeth Landon (1802–1838)

April

LINES 1–13

'THE SPRING COMES SLOWLY UP THIS WAY'

CHRISTABEL

'Tis the noon of the spring-time, yet never a bird
In the wind-shaken elm or the maple is heard;
For green meadow-grasses wide levels of snow,
And blowing of drifts where the crocus should blow;
Where wind-flower and violet, amber and white,
On south-sloping brooksides should smile in the light,
O'er the cold winter-beds of their late-waking roots
The frosty flake eddies, the ice-crystal shoots;
And, longing for light, under wind-driven heaps,
Round the boles of the pine-wood the ground-laurel creeps,
Unkissed of the sunshine, unbaptized of showers,
With buds scarcely swelled, which should burst into flowers!
We wait for thy coming, sweet wind of the south!

John Greenleaf Whittier (1807–1892)

Beachy Head

LINES 346–367

An early worshipper at nature's shrine,
I loved her rudest scenes – warrens, and heaths,
And yellow commons, and birch-shaded hollows,
And hedgerows, bordering unfrequented lanes,
Bowered with wild roses, and the clasping woodbine
Where purple tassels of the tangling vetch
With bittersweet, and bryony inweave,
And the dew fills the silver bindweed's cups –
I loved to trace the brooks whose humid banks
Nourish the harebell, and the freckled pagil;
And stroll among o'ershadowing woods of beech,
Lending in summer, from the heats of noon
A whispering shade; while haply there reclines
Some pensive lover of uncultured flowers,
Who, from the tumps with bright green mosses clad,
Plucks the wood-sorrel, with its light thin leaves,
Heart-shaped, and triply-folded; and its root
Creeping like beaded coral; or who there
Gathers, the copse's pride, anemones,
With rays like golden studs on ivory laid
Most delicate: but touched with purple clouds,
Fit crown for April's fair but changeful brow.

Charlotte Smith (1749–1806)

7 APRIL

Put Forth Thy Leaf

Put forth thy leaf, thou lofty plane,
  East wind and frost are safely gone;
With zephyr mild and balmy rain
  The summer comes serenely on;
Earth, air, and sun and skies combine
  To promise all that's kind and fair: –
But thou, O human heart of mine,
  Be still, contain thyself, and bear.

December days were brief and chill,
  The winds of March were wild and drear,
And, nearing and receding still,
  Spring never would, we thought, be here.
The leaves that burst, the suns that shine,
  Had, not the less, their certain date: –
And thou, O human heart of mine,
  Be still, refrain thyself, and wait.

Arthur Hugh Clough (1819–1861)

Night

night finds us, creeping soundlessly
past window pane, through door ajar:
and not even a candle's glow
can halt the irredeeming course.

the curtains drawn prevent the skulk
of dark's advance, but not too much:
the night expands and we accept
its scalding web, with no remorse.

Joel Knight (1975–)

The Crow

With rakish eye and plenished crop,
  Oblivious of the farmer's gun,
Upon the naked ash-tree top
  The Crow sits basking in the sun.

An old ungodly rogue, I wot!
  For, perched in black against the blue,
His feathers, torn with beak and shot,
  Let woeful glints of April through.

The year's new grass, and, golden-eyed,
  The daisies sparkle underneath,
And chestnut-trees on either side
  Have opened every ruddy sheath.

But doubtful still of frost and snow,
  The ash alone stands stark and bare,
And on its topmost twig the Crow
  Takes the glad morning's sun and air.

William Canton (1845–1926)

After the Winter

Some day, when trees have shed their leaves
    And against the morning's white
The shivering birds beneath the eaves
    Have sheltered for the night,
We'll turn our faces southward, love,
    Toward the summer isle
Where bamboos spire the shafted grove
    And wide-mouthed orchids smile.

And we will seek the quiet hill
    Where towers the cotton tree,
And leaps the laughing crystal rill,
    And works the droning bee.
And we will build a cottage there
    Beside an open glade,
With black-ribbed blue-bells blowing near,
    And ferns that never fade.

Claude McKay (1890–1948)

The Birds and the Flowers

FROM *MILTON*, LINES 1–18

Thou hearest the Nightingale begin the Song of Spring:
The Lark, sitting upon his earthy bed, just as the morn
Appears, listens silent; then, springing from the waving corn-field, loud
He leads the Choir of Day – trill! trill! trill! trill!
Mounting upon the wings of light into the great Expanse,
Re-echoing against the lovely blue and shining heavenly Shell;
His little throat labours with inspiration; every feather
On throat and breast and wings vibrates with the effluence Divine.
All Nature listens to him silent, and the awful Sun
Stands still upon the mountains, looking on this little Bird
With eyes of soft humility and wonder, love and awe.
Then loud, from their green covert, all the Birds begin their song:
The Thrush, the Linnet and the Goldfinch, Robin and the Wren,
Awake the Sun from his sweet reverie upon the mountain:
The Nightingale again essays his song, and thro' the day
And thro'the night warbles luxuriant; every Bird of song
Attending his loud harmony with admiration and love.
This is a Vision of the lamentation of Beulah over Ololon.

William Blake (1757–1827)

Afton Water

Flow gently, sweet Afton, among thy green braes,
Flow gently, I'll sing thee a song in thy praise;
My Mary's asleep by thy murmuring stream,
Flow gently, sweet Afton, disturb not her dream.

Thou stock-dove, whose echo resounds thro' the glen,
Ye wild whistling blackbirds in yon thorny den,
Thou green-crested lapwing, thy screaming forbear,
I charge you disturb not my slumbering fair.

How lofty, sweet Afton, thy neighbouring hills,
Far mark'd with the courses of clear winding rills;
There daily I wander as noon rises high,
My flocks and my Mary's sweet cot in my eye.

How pleasant thy banks and green valleys below,
Where wild in the woodlands the primroses blow;
There oft, as mild ev'ning sweeps over the lea,
The sweet-scented birk shades my Mary and me.

Thy crystal stream, Afton, how lovely it glides,
And winds by the cot where my Mary resides,
How wanton thy waters her snowy feet lave,
As gathering sweet flowrets she stems thy clear wave.

Flow gently, sweet Afton, among thy green braes,
Flow gently, sweet river, the theme of my lays;
My Mary's asleep by thy murmuring stream,
Flow gently, sweet Afton, disturb not her dream.

Robert Burns (1759–1796)

Buds

The raining hour is done,
        And, threaded on the bough,
The may-buds in the sun
        Are shining emeralds now.

As transitory these
        As things of April will,
Yet, trembling in the trees,
        Is briefer beauty still.

For, flowering from the sky
        Upon an April day,
Are silver buds that lie
        Amid the buds of may.

The April emeralds now,
        While thrushes fill the lane,
Are linked along the bough
        With silver buds of rain.

And, straightly though to earth
        The buds of silver slip,
The green buds keep the mirth
        Of that companionship.

John Drinkwater (1882–1937)

Repeat that, Repeat

Repeat that, repeat,
Cuckoo, bird, and open ear wells, heart-springs,
  delightfully sweet,
With a ballad, with a ballad, a rebound
Off trundled timber and scoops of the hillside ground,
  hollow hollow hollow ground:
The whole landscape flushes on a sudden at a sound.

Gerard Manley Hopkins (1844–1889)

April

A bird chirped at my window this morning,
And over the sky is drawn a light network of clouds.
Come,
Let us go out into the open,
For my heart leaps like a fish that is ready to spawn.

I will lie under the beech-trees,
Under the grey branches of the beech-trees,
In a blueness of little squills and crocuses.
I will lie among the little squills
And be delivered of this overcharge of beauty,
And that which is born shall be a joy to you
Who love me.

Amy Lowell (1874–1925)

Bird Raptures

The sunrise wakes the lark to sing,
  The moonrise wakes the nightingale.
Come darkness, moonrise, everything
  That is so silent, sweet, and pale,
  Come, so ye wake the nightingale.

Make haste to mount, thou wistful moon,
  Make haste to wake the nightingale:
Let silence set the world in tune
  To hearken to that wordless tale
  Which warbles from the nightingale.

O herald skylark, stay thy flight
  One moment, for a nightingale
Floods us with sorrow and delight.
  To-morrow thou shalt hoist the sail;
  Leave us tonight the nightingale.

Christina Rossetti (1830–1894)

I Wandered Lonely as a Cloud

WRITTEN AT TOWN-END, GRASMERE.

I wandered lonely as a cloud
That floats on high o'er vales and hills,
When all at once I saw a crowd,
A host, of golden daffodils;
Beside the lake, beneath the trees,
Fluttering and dancing in the breeze.

Continuous as the stars that shine
And twinkle on the milky way,
They stretched in never-ending line
Along the margin of the bay:
Ten thousand saw I at a glance,
Tossing their heads in sprightly dance.

The waves beside them danced; but they
Out-did the sparkling waves in glee:
A poet could not but be gay,
In such a jocund company:
I gazed – and gazed – but little thought
What wealth the show to me had brought:

For oft, when on my couch I lie
In vacant or in pensive mood,
They flash upon that inward eye
Which is the bliss of solitude;
And then my heart with pleasure fills,
And dances with the daffodils.

William Wordsworth (1770–1850)

The Loveliest of Trees

A SHROPSHIRE LAD, II

Loveliest of trees, the cherry now
Is hung with bloom along the bough,
And stands about the woodlands ride
Wearing white for Eastertide.

Now, of my threescore years and ten,
Twenty will not come again,
And take from seventy springs a score,
It only leaves me fifty more.

And since to look at things in bloom
Fifty springs are little room,
About the woodlands I will go
To see the cherry hung with snow.

A. E. Housman (1859–1936)

Quails Nest

I wandered out one rainy day
And heard a bird with merry joys
Cry 'wet my foot' for half the way
I stood and wondered at the noise

When from my foot a bird did flee
The rain flew bouncing from her breast
I wondered what the bird could be
And almost trampled on her nest

The nest was full of eggs and round
I met a shepherd in the vales
And stood to tell him what I found.
He knew and said it was a quails

For he himself the nest had found
Among the wheat and on the green
When going on his daily round
With eggs as many as fifteen

Among the stranger birds they feed
Their summer flight is short and low
Theres very few know where they breed
And scarcely any where they go

John Clare (1793–1864)

A Flower of the Himalayas

A flower of the Himalayas
on this Welsh hillside, says its prayers.
A flower from another land
is trying to make us understand.
Its prayers, though they be Hindu
are yet the same,
for me and you.

David Austin (1926–2018)

Apple Blossoms

Amid the young year's breathing hopes,
  When eager grasses wrap the earth,
I see on greening orchard slopes
  The blossoms trembling into birth.
They open wide their rosy palms
  To feel the hesitating rain,
Or beg a longed-for golden alms
  From skies that deep in clouds have lain.

They mingle with the bluebird's songs,
  And with the warm wind's reverie;
To sward and stream their snow belongs,
  To neighboring pines in flocks they flee,
O doubly crowned with breathing hopes
  The branches bending down to earth
That feel on greening orchard slopes
  Their blossoms trembling into birth!

Ethelwyn Wetherald (1857–1940)

Thyrsis

A MONODY, TO COMMEMORATE THE AUTHOR'S FRIEND,
ARTHUR HUGH CLOUGH, WHO DIED AT FLORENCE, 1861
VERSE 12

I know these slopes; who knows them if not I? –
But many a dingle on the loved hill-side,
With thorns once studded, old, white-blossom'd trees,
Where thick the cowslips grew, and far descried
High tower'd the spikes of purple orchises,
Hath since our day put by
The coronals of that forgotten time;
Down each green bank hath gone the ploughboy's team,
And only in the hidden brookside gleam
Primroses, orphans of the flowery prime.

Matthew Arnold (1822–1888)

Hark, Hark, the Lark

FROM *CYMBELINE*, ACT II, SCENE III

Hark, hark, the lark at heaven gate sings,
        And Phoebus gins arise,
His steeds to water at those springs
    On chaliced flowers that lies,
And winking Mary-buds begin to ope their golden eyes;
With everything that pretty is, my lady sweet, arise,
        Arise, arise!

William Shakespeare (1564–1616)

The Nightingale

A CONVERSATION POEM, APRIL, 1798

LINES 1–39

No cloud, no relique of the sunken day
Distinguishes the West, no long thin slip
Of sullen light, no obscure trembling hues.
Come, we will rest on this old mossy bridge!
You see the glimmer of the stream beneath,
But hear no murmuring: it flows silently.
O'er its soft bed of verdure. All is still.
A balmy night! and though the stars be dim,
Yet let us think upon the vernal showers
That gladden the green earth, and we shall find
A pleasure in the dimness of the stars.
And hark! the Nightingale begins its song,
'Most musical, most melancholy' bird!
A melancholy bird? Oh! idle thought!
In Nature there is nothing melancholy.
But some night-wandering man whose heart was pierced
With the remembrance of a grievous wrong,
Or slow distemper, or neglected love,
(And so, poor wretch! filled all things with himself,
And made all gentle sounds tell back the tale
Of his own sorrow) he, and such as he,
First named these notes a melancholy strain.
And many a poet echoes the conceit;
Poet who hath been building up the rhyme
When he had better far have stretched his limbs

Beside a brook in mossy forest-dell,
By sun or moon-light, to the influxes
Of shapes and sounds and shifting elements
Surrendering his whole spirit, of his song
And of his fame forgetful! so his fame
Should share in Nature's immortality,
A venerable thing! and so his song
Should make all Nature lovelier, and itself
Be loved like Nature! But 'twill not be so;
And youths and maidens most poetical,
Who lose the deepening twilights of the spring
In ball-rooms and hot theatres, they still
Full of meek sympathy must heave their sighs
O'er Philomela's pity-pleading strains.

Samuel Taylor Coleridge (1772–1834)

April's Charms

When April scatters coins of primrose gold
Among the copper leaves in thickets old,
And singing skylarks from the meadows rise,
To twinkle like black stars in sunny skies;

When I can hear the small woodpecker ring
Time on a tree for all the birds that sing;
And hear the pleasant cuckoo, loud and long –
The simple bird that thinks two notes a song;

When I can hear the woodland brook, that could
Not drown a babe, with all his threatening mood;
Upon these banks the violets make their home,
And let a few small strawberry blossoms come:

When I go forth on such a pleasant day,
One breath outdoors takes all my cares away;
It goes like heavy smoke, when flames take hold
Of wood that's green and fill a grate with gold.

W. H. Davies (1871–1940)

Bluebells

Like smoke held down by frost
The bluebells wreathe in the wood.
Spring like a swan there
Feeds on a cold flood:

But the winter woodmen know
How to make flame
From sodden December faggots,
They can make the blue smoke climb.

Picked flowers wilt at once,
They flare but where they are;
The swan will not sing nor the fire thrive
In a town-watered jar:

But the winter woodmen know
The essential secret burning;
The fire at the earth's core
In touch with the turning sun.

Patric Dickinson (1914–1994)

The Shepheardes Calender, Aprill

LINES 136–144

Bring hether the Pincke and purple Cullambine,
With Gelliflowres:
Bring Coronations, and Sops in wine,
worne of Paramoures.
Strowe me the ground with Daffadowndillies,
And Cowslips, and Kingcups, and loved Lillies:
The pretie Pawnce,
And the Cheuisaunce,
Shall match with the fayre flowre Delice.

Edmund Spenser (c.1552–1599)

March Strongly Forth

FROM *POLY-OLBION*, SONG II, LINES 1–18

March strongly forth, my Muse, whilst yet the temperate air
Invites us easily on to hasten our repair.
Thou powerful god of flames (in verse divinely great)
Touch my invention so with thy true genuine heat
That high and noble things I slightly may not tell,
Nor light and idle toys my lines may vainly swell;
But, as my subject serves, so high or low to strain,
And to the varying earth so suit my varying vein,
That, nature, in my work thou mayst thy power avow;
That, as thou first foundst art and didst her rules allow,
So I, to thine own self that gladly near would be,
May herein do the best, in imitating thee.
As thou hast here a hill, a vale there, there a flood,
A mead here, there a heath, and now and then a wood,
These things so in my song I naturally may show:
Now as the mountain high, then as the valley low;
Here fruitful as the mead, there as the heath be bare;
Then, as the gloomy wood, I may be rough, though rare.

Michael Drayton (1563–1631)

Parta Quies

Good-night; ensured release,
Imperishable peace,
        Have these for yours,
While sea abides, and land,
And earth's foundations stand,
        And heaven endures.

When earth's foundations flee,
Nor sky nor land nor sea
        At all is found,
Content you, let them burn:
It is not your concern;
        Sleep on, sleep sound.

A. E. Housman (1859–1936)

The April Sky Sags Low and Drear

PRAELUDIUM, VII

The April sky sags low and drear,
  The April winds blow cold,
The April rains fall gray and sheer,
  And yeanlings keep the fold.

But the rook has built, and the song-birds quire,
  And over the faded lea
The lark soars glorying, gyre on gyre,
  And he is the bird for me!

For he sings as if from his watchman's height
  He saw, this blighting day,
The far vales break into colour and light
  From the banners and arms of May.

W. E. Henley (1849–1903)

MAY

The Moon Shines White and Silent

Night of Frost in May

LINES 1–14

With splendour of a silver day,
A frosted night had opened May:
And on that plumed and armoured night,
As one close temple hove our wood,
Its border leafage virgin white.
Remote down air an owl hallooed.
The black twig dropped without a twirl;
The bud in jewelled grasp was nipped;
The brown leaf cracked a scorching curl;
A crystal off the green leaf slipped.
Across the tracks of rimy tan,
Some busy thread at whiles would shoot;
A limping minnow-rillet ran,
To hang upon an icy foot.

George Meredith (1828–1909)

The Cloud

One could not see or think, the heat overcame one,
With a dazzle of square road to challenge and blind one,
No water was there, cow-parsley the only flower
Of all May's garland this torrid before summer hour,
And but one ploughman to break ten miles of solitariness.
No water, water to drink, stare at, the lovely clean grained one.

Where like a falcon on prey, shadow flung downward
Solid as gun-metal, the eyes sprang sunward
To salute the silver radiance of an Atlantic high
Prince of vapour required of the retinue
Continual changing of the outer-sea's flooding sun
Cloud royal, born called and ordered to domination,
Spring called him out of his tent in the azure of pleasure,
He girt his nobleness – and in slow pace went onward
A true monarch of air chosen to service and station;
And directed on duties of patrolling the considered blue.
But what his course required being fulfilled, what fancy
Of beyond-imagination did his power escape to
With raiment of blown silver ...

Ivor Gurney (1890–1937)

Sonnet

After dark vapors have oppress'd our plains
  For a long dreary season, comes a day
  Born of the gentle South, and clears away
From the sick heavens all unseemly stains.
The anxious month, relieved of its pains,
  Takes as a long-lost right the feel of May;
  The eyelids with the passing coolness play
Like rose leaves with the drip of Summer rains.
The calmest thoughts came round us; as of leaves
Budding – fruit ripening in stillness – Autumn suns
  Smiling at eve upon the quiet sheaves –
Sweet Sappho's cheek – a smiling infant's breath –
  The gradual sand that through an hour-glass runs –
A woodland rivulet – a Poet's death.

John Keats (1795–1821)

The Trees

The trees are coming into leaf
Like something almost being said;
The recent buds relax and spread,
Their greenness is a kind of grief.

Is it that they are born again
And we grow old? No, they die too,
Their yearly trick of looking new
Is written down in rings of grain.

Yet still the unresting castles thresh
In fullgrown thickness every May.
Last year is dead, they seem to say,
Begin afresh, afresh, afresh.

Philip Larkin (1922–1985)

Voices of the Night

PRELUDE, VERSES 1–4

Pleasant it was, when woods were green
 And winds were soft and low,
To lie amid some sylvan scene,
Where, the long drooping boughs between,
Shadows dark and sunlight sheen
 Alternate come and go;

Or where the denser grove receives
 No sunlight from above,
But the dark foliage interweaves
In one unbroken roof of leaves,
Underneath whose sloping eaves
 The shadows hardly move.

Beneath some patriarchal tree
 I lay upon the ground;
His hoary arms uplifted he,
And all the broad leaves over me
Clapped their little hands in glee,
 With one continuous sound; –

A slumberous sound, a sound that brings
 The feelings of a dream,
As of innumerable wings,
As, when a bell no longer swings,
Faint the hollow murmur rings
 O'er meadow, lake, and stream.

Henry Wadsworth Longfellow (1807–1882)

Midnight

The moon shines white and silent
  On the mist, which, like a tide
Of some enchanted ocean,
  O'er the wide marsh doth glide,
Spreading its ghost-like billows
  Silently far and wide.

A vague and starry magic
  Makes all things mysteries,
And lures the earth's dumb spirit
  Up to the longing skies, –
I seem to hear dim whispers,
  And tremulous replies.

The fireflies o'er the meadow
  In pulses come and go;
The elm-trees' heavy shadow
  Weighs on the grass below;
And faintly from the distance
  The dreaming cock doth crow.

All things look strange and mystic,
  The very bushes swell
And take wild shapes and motions,
  As if beneath a spell;
They seem not the same lilacs
  From childhood known so well.

The snow of deepest silence
  O'er everything doth fall,
So beautiful and quiet,
  And yet so like a pall;
As if all life were ended,
  And rest were come to all.

O wild and wondrous midnight,
  There is a might in thee
To make the charmèd body
  Almost like spirit be,
And give it some faint glimpses
  Of immortality!

James Russell Lowell (1819–1891)

The Mystery

If sunset clouds could grow on trees
It would but match the may in flower;
And skies be underneath the seas
No topsyturvier than a shower.

If mountains rose on wings to wander
They were no wilder than a cloud;
Yet all my praise is mean as slander,
Mean as these mean words spoken aloud.

And never more than now I know
That man's first heaven is far behind;
Unless the blazing seraph's blow
Has left him in the garden blind.

Witness, O Sun that blinds our eyes,
Unthinkable and unthankable King,
That though all other wonder dies
I wonder at not wondering.

G. K. Chesterton (1874–1936)

The Lilac is in Bloom

FROM 'THE OLD VICARAGE, GRANTCHESTER'
(CAFÉ DES WESTENS, BERLIN, MAY 1912)

Just now the lilac is in bloom,
All before my little room;
And in my flower-beds, I think,
Smile the carnations and the pink;
And down the borders, well I know,
The poppy and the pansy blow ...
Oh! there the chestnuts, summer through,
Beside the river make for you
A tunnel of green gloom, and sleep
Deeply above; and green and deep
The stream mysterious glides beneath,
Green as a dream and deep as death.
– Oh, damn! I know it! and I know
How the May fields all golden show,
And when the day is young and sweet,
Gild gloriously the bare feet
That run to bathe ...

Ah God! to see the branches stir
Across the moon at Grantchester!
To smell the thrilling-sweet and rotten
Unforgettable, unforgotten
River-smell, and hear the breeze
Sobbing in the little trees.
Say, do the elm-clumps greatly stand
Still guardians of that holy land?

The chestnuts shade, in reverend dream,
The yet unacademic stream?
Is dawn a secret shy and cold
Anadyomene, silver and gold?
And sunset still a golden sea
From Haslingfield to Madingley?
And after, ere the night is born,
Do hares come out about the corn?
Oh, is the water sweet and cool,
Gentle and brown, above the pool?
And laughs the immortal river still
Under the mill, under the mill?
Say, is there Beauty yet to find?
And Certainty? and Quiet kind?
Deep meadows yet, for to forget
The lies, and truths, and pain? ...oh! yet
Stands the Church clock at ten to three?
And is there honey still for tea?

Rupert Brooke (1887–1915)

The Green Linnet

Beneath these fruit-tree boughs that shed
Their snow-white blossoms on my head,
With brightest sunshine round me spread
Of spring's unclouded weather,
In this sequestered nook how sweet
To sit upon my orchard-seat!
And birds and flowers once more to greet,
My last year's friends together.

One have I marked, the happiest guest
In all this covert of the blest:
Hail to Thee, far above the rest
In joy of voice and pinion!
Thou, Linnet! in thy green array,
Presiding Spirit here to-day,
Dost lead the revels of the May;
And this is thy dominion.

While birds, and butterflies, and flowers,
Make all one band of paramours,
Thou, ranging up and down the bowers,
Art sole in thy employment:
A Life, a Presence like the Air,
Scattering thy gladness without care,
Too blest with any one to pair;
Thyself thy own enjoyment.

Amid yon tuft of hazel trees,
That twinkle to the gusty breeze,
Behold him perched in ecstasies,
  Yet seeming still to hover;
There! where the flutter of his wings
Upon his back and body flings
Shadows and sunny glimmerings,
  That cover him all over.

My dazzled sight he oft deceives,
A brother of the dancing leaves;
Then flits, and from the cottage-eaves
  Pours forth his song in gushes;
As if by that exulting strain
He mocked and treated with disdain
The voiceless Form he chose to feign,
  While fluttering in the bushes.

William Wordsworth (1770–1850)

The Vision of Piers Plowman

PROLOGUE, LINES 1–10

In a somer sesun whan soft was the sonne,
I shope me in shroudes as I a shepe were;
In habite as an heremite unholy of workes
Went wyde in this world wondres to here.
Ac on a May mornynge on Malverne hulles
Me byfel a ferly of fairy, me thoughte;
I was wery forwandred and went me to reste
Undur a brod banke bi a bornes side,
And as I lay and lened and loked in the watres,
I slombred in a slepyng it sweyued so merye.

William Langland (c.1332–c.1400)

The First Dandelion

Simple and fresh and fair from winter's close emerging,
As if no artifice of fashion, business, politics, had ever been,
Forth from its sunny nook of shelter'd grass – innocent, golden,
        calm as the dawn,
The spring's first dandelion shows its trustful face.

Walt Whitman (1819–1892)

Ode to a Nightingale

VERSES I–IV

I

My heart aches, and a drowsy numbness pains
My sense, as though of hemlock I had drunk,
Or emptied some dull opiate to the drains
One minute past, and Lethe-wards had sunk:
'Tis not through envy of thy happy lot,
But being too happy in thine happiness, –
That thou, light-winged Dryad of the trees,
In some melodious plot
Of beechen green, and shadows numberless,
Singest of summer in full-throated ease.

II

O, for a draught of vintage! that hath been
Cool'd a long age in the deep-delved earth,
Tasting of Flora and the country green,
Dance, and Provençal song, and sunburnt mirth!
O for a beaker full of the warm South,
Full of the true, the blushful Hippocrene,
With beaded bubbles winking at the brim,
And purple-stained mouth;
That I might drink, and leave the world unseen,
And with thee fade away into the forest dim:

II

Fade far away, dissolve, and quite forget
  What thou among the leaves hast never known,
The weariness, the fever, and the fret
  Here, where men sit and hear each other groan;
Where palsy shakes a few, sad, last grey hairs,
  Where youth grows pale, and spectre-thin, and dies;
    Where but to think is to be full of sorrow
      And leaden-eyed despairs,
  Where Beauty cannot keep her lustrous eyes,
    Or new Love pine at them beyond to-morrow

IV

Away! away! for I will fly to thee,
  Not charioted by Bacchus and his pards,
But on the viewless wings of Poesy,
  Though the dull brain perplexes and retards:
Already with thee! tender is the night,
  And haply the Queen-Moon is on her throne,
    Cluster'd around by all her starry Fays;
      But here there is no light,
  Save what from heaven is with the breezes blown
    Through verdurous glooms and winding mossy ways.

John Keats (1795–1821)

A Brilliant Day

O keen pellucid air! nothing can lurk
Or disavow itself on this bright day;
The small rain-plashes shine from far away,
The tiny emmet glitters at his work;
The bee looks blithe and gay, and as she plies
Her task, and moves and sidles round the cup
Of this spring flower, to drink its honey up,
Her glassy wings, like oars that dip and rise,
Gleam momently. Pure-bosomed, clear of fog,
The long lake glistens, while the glorious beam
Bespangles the wet joints and floating leaves
Of water-plants, whose every point receives
His light; and jellies of the spawning frog,
Unmarked before, like piles of jewels seem!

Charles Tennyson Turner (1808–1879)

Nightingales

Beautiful must be the mountains whence ye come,
And bright in the fruitful valleys the streams, wherefrom
Ye learn your song:
Where are those starry woods? O might I wander there,
Among the flowers, which in that heavenly air
Bloom the year long!

Nay, barren are those mountains and spent the streams:
Our song is the voice of desire, that haunts our dreams,
A throe of the heart,
Whose pining visions dim, forbidden hopes profound,
No dying cadence, nor long sigh can sound,
For all our art.

Alone, aloud in the raptured ear of men
We pour our dark nocturnal secret; and then,
As night is withdrawn
From these sweet-springing meads and bursting boughs of May,
Dream, while the innumerable choir of day
Welcome the dawn.

Robert Bridges (1844–1930)

Hedges

'Bread and cheese' grow wild in the green time,
  Children laugh and pick it, and I make my rhyme
For mere pleasure of seeing that so subtle play,
  Of arms and various legs going every, any, other way.

And they turn and laugh for the unexpensiveness
  Of country grocery and are pleased no less
Than hedge sparrows. Lessons will be easier taken,
  For this gypsy chaffering, the hedge plucked and green shaken.

Ivor Gurney (1890–1937)

The Lily of the Valley

Some flowers there are that rear their heads on high,
The gorgeous products of a burning sky,
That rush upon the eye with garish bloom,
And make the senses drunk with high perfume.
Not such art thou, sweet Lily of the Vale!
So lovely, small, and delicately pale, –
We might believe, if such fond faith were ours,
As sees humanity in trees and flowers,
That thou wert once a maiden, meek and good,
That pined away beneath her native wood
For very fear of her own loveliness,
And died of love she never would confess.

Hartley Coleridge (1796–1849)

Ode: On the Spring

VERSES 1–3

Lo! where the rosy-bosom'd Hours,
  Fair Venus' train appear,
Disclose the long-expecting flowers,
  And wake the purple year!
The Attic warbler pours her throat,
Responsive to the cuckoo's note,
  The untaught harmony of spring:
While, whisp'ring pleasure as they fly,
Cool Zephyrs thro' the clear blue sky
  Their gather'd fragrance fling.

Where'er the oak's thick branches stretch
  A broader browner shade;
Where'er the rude and moss-grown beech
  O'er-canopies the glade,
Beside some water's rushy brink
With me the Muse shall sit, and think
  (At ease reclin'd in rustic state)
How vain the ardour of the crowd,
How low, how little are the proud,
  How indigent the great!

Still is the toiling hand of Care;
  The panting herds repose:
Yet hark, how thro' the peopled air
  The busy murmur glows!
The insect-youth are on the wing,
Eager to taste the honied spring,
  And float amid the liquid noon:
Some lightly o'er the current skim,
Some show their gayly-gilded trim
  Quick-glancing to the sun.

Thomas Gray (1716–1771)

Golden Glories

The buttercup is like a golden cup,
  The marigold is like a golden frill,
The daisy with a golden eye looks up,
  And golden spreads the flag beside the rill,
  And gay and golden nods the daffodil,
The gorsey common swells a golden sea,
  The cowslip hangs a head of golden tips,
And golden drips the honey which the bee
  Sucks from sweet hearts of flowers and stores and sips.

Christina Rossetti (1830–1894)

The Nightingale

O nightingale, that on yon bloomy spray
  Warblest at eve, when all the woods are still,
  Thou with fresh hope the lover's heart dost fill,
  While the jolly hours lead on propitious May,
Thy liquid notes that close the eye of day,
  First heard before the shallow cuckoo's bill
  Portend success in love. O, if Jove's will
  Have linked that amorous power to thy soft lay,
Now timely sing, ere the rude bird of hate
  Foretell my hopeless doom in some grove nigh,
  As thou from year to year hast sung too late
For my relief, yet hadst no reason why,
  Whether the Muse or Love call thee his mate
  Both them I serve, and of their train am I.

John Milton (1608–1674)

May, 1915

Let us remember Spring will come again
To the scorched, blackened woods, where the wounded trees
Wait, with their old wise patience for the heavenly rain,
Sure of the sky: sure of the sea to send its healing breeze,
Sure of the sun. And even as to these
Surely the Spring, when God shall please,
Will come again like a divine surprise
To those who sit to-day with their great Dead, hands in their hands, eyes in their eyes,
At one with Love, at one with Grief: blind to the scattered things and changing skies.

Charlotte Mew (1869–1928)

21 MAY

Nocturnal Reverie

LINES 1 18

In such a night, when every louder wind
Is to its distant cavern safe confined;
And only gentle Zephyr fans his wings,
And lonely Philomel, still waking, sings;
Or from some tree, famed for the owl's delight,
She, hollowing clear, directs the wanderer right:
In such a night, when passing clouds give place,
Or thinly veil the heavens' mysterious face;
When in some river, overhung with green,
The waving moon and the trembling leaves are seen;
When freshened grass now bears itself upright,
And makes cool banks to pleasing rest invite,
Whence springs the woodbind, and the bramble-rose,
And where the sleepy cowslip sheltered grows;
Whilst now a paler hue the foxglove takes,
Yet checkers still with red the dusky brakes
When scattered glow-worms, but in twilight fine,
Show trivial beauties, watch their hour to shine;

Anne Finch, Countess of Winchelsea (1661–1720)

The Enviable Isles

Through storms you reach them and from storms are free.
  Afar descried, the foremost drear in hue,
But, nearer, green; and, on the marge, the sea
  Makes thunder low and mist of rainbowed dew.

But, inland, where the sleep that folds the hills
A dreamier sleep, the trance of God, instills –
  On uplands hazed, in wandering airs aswoon,
Slow-swaying palms salute love's cypress tree
  Adown in vale where pebbly runlets croon
A song to lull all sorrow and all glee.

Sweet-fern and moss in many a glade are here.
  Where, strewn in flocks, what cheek-flushed myriads lie
Dimpling in dream – unconscious slumberers mere,
  While billows endless round the beaches die.

Herman Melville (1819–1891)

23 MAY

The Legend of Good Women

PROLOGUE, LINES 40–50

Now have I therto this condicioun
That, of alle the floures in the mede,
Than love I most these floures whyte and rede,
Swiche as men callen daysies in our toun.
To hem have I so greet affeccioun,
As I seyde erst, whan comen is the May,
That in my bed ther daweth me no day
That I nam up, and walking in the mede
To seen these floures agein the sonne sprede,
Whan it up-riseth by the morwe shene,
The longe day, thus walking in the grene.

Geoffrey Chaucer (c.1343–1400)

The Vixen

Among the taller wood with ivy hung
The old fox plays and dances round her young
She snuffs and barks if any passes bye
And swings her tail and turns prepared to flye
The horseman hurries bye she bolts to see
And turns agen from danger never free
If any stands she runs among the poles
And barks and snaps and drive them in the holes
The shepherd sees them and the boy goes bye
And gets a stick and progs the hole to try
They get all still and lie in safty sure
And out again when safety is secure
And start and snap at blackbirds bouncing by
To fight and catch the great white butterflye

John Clare (1793–1864)

25 MAY

Proportion

In the sky there is a moon and stars
And in my garden there are yellow moths
Fluttering about a white azalea bush.

Amy Lowell (1874–1925)

Sedge-warblers

This beauty made me dream there was a time
Long past and irrecoverable, a clime
Where any brook so radiant racing clear
Through buttercup and kingcup bright as brass
But gentle, nourishing the meadow grass
That leans and scurries in the wind, would bear
Another beauty, divine and feminine,
Child to the sun, a nymph whose soul unstained
Could love all day, and never hate or tire,
A lover of mortal or immortal kin.

And yet, rid of this dream, ere I had drained
Its poison, quieted was my desire
So that I only looked into the water,
Clearer than any goddess or man's daughter,
And hearkened while it combed the dark green hair
And shook the millions of the blossoms white
Of water-crowfoot, and curdled to one sheet
The flowers fallen from the chestnuts in the park
Far off. And sedge-warblers, clinging so light
To willow twigs, sang longer than the lark,
Quick, shrill, or grating, a song to match the heat
Of the strong sun, nor less the water's cool,
Gushing through narrows, swirling in the pool.

Their song that lacks all words, all melody,
All sweetness almost, was dearer then to me
Than sweetest voice that sings in tune sweet words.
This was the best of May – the small brown birds
Wisely reiterating endlessly
What no man learnt yet, in or out of school.

Edward Thomas (1878–1917)

O were my Love yon Lilac fair

O were my love yon lilac fair,
Wi' purple blossoms to the spring,
And I, a bird to shelter there,
When wearied on my little wing;

How I wad mourn when it was torn
By autumn wild, and winter rude!
But I wad sing on wanton wing,
When youthfu' May its bloom renew'd.

O gin my love were yon red rose,
That grows upon the castle wa',
And I mysel' a drap o' dew,
Into her bonie breast to fa'!

Oh, there beyond expression blest,
I'd feast on beauty a' the night;
Seal'd on her silk-saft faulds to rest,
Till fley'd awa' by Phoebus' light.

Robert Burns (1759–1796)

May Evening

So late the rustling shower was heard;
Yet now the aëry west is still.
The wet leaves flash, and lightly stirred
Great drops out of the lilac spill.
Peacefully blown, the ashen clouds
Uncurtain height on height of sky.
Here, as I wander, beauty crowds
In freshness keen upon my eye.

Now the shorn turf a glowing green
Takes in the massy cedar shade;
And through the poplar's trembling screen
Fires of the evening blush and fade.
Each way my marvelling senses feel
Swift odour, light, and luminous hue
Of leaf and flower upon them steal:
The songs of birds pierce my heart through.

The tulip clear, like yellow flame,
Burns upward from the gloomy mould:
As though for passion forth they came,
Red hearts of peonies unfold:
And perfumes tender, sweet, intense
Enter me, delicate as a blade.
The lilac odour wounds my sense,
Of the rich rose I am afraid.

Laurence Binyon (1869–1943)

Of Many Worlds in this World

Just like unto a nest of boxes round,
Degrees of sizes within each box are found,
So, in this world, may many worlds more be,
Thinner, and less, and less still by degree;
Although they are not subject to our sense,
A world may be no bigger than twopence.
Nature is curious, and such work may make
That our dull sense can never find, but scape.
For creatures small as atoms may be there,
If every atom a creature's figure bear.
If four atoms a world can make, then see
What several worlds might in an ear-ring be.
For millions of those atoms may be in
The head of one small, little, single pin.
And if thus small, then ladies may well wear
A world of worlds as pendents in each ear.

Margaret Cavendish (1623–1673)

In the Heart of the Forest

VERSES I–VIII

I

I heard the voice of my own true love
  Ripple the sunny weather.
Then away, as a dove that follows a dove,
  We flitted through woods together.

II

There was not a bush nor branch nor spray
  But with song was swaying and ringing.
'Let us ask of the birds what means their lay,
  And what is it prompts their singing.'

III

We paused where the stichwort and speedwell grew
  'Mid a forest of grasses fairy:
From out of the covert the cushat flew,
  And the squirrel perched shy and wary.

IV

On an elm-tree top shrilled a misselthrush proud,
  Disdaining shelter or screening.
'Now what is it makes you pipe so loud,
  And what is your music's meaning?

V

'Your matins begin ere the dewdrop sinks
  To the heart of the moist musk-roses,
And your vespers last till the first star winks,
  And the vigilant woodreeve dozes.'

VI

Then louder, still louder he shrilled: 'I sing
For the pleasure and pride of shrilling,
For the sheen and the sap and the showers of Spring
That fill me to overfilling.

VII

'Yet a something deeper than Spring-time, though
It is Spring-like, my throat keeps flooding:
Peep soft at my mate, – she is there below, –
Where the bramble trails are budding.

VIII

'She sits on the nest and she never stirs;
She is true to the trust I gave her;
And what were my love if I cheered not hers
As long as my throat can quaver?'

Alfred Austin (1835–1913)

The Birds and the Flowers

FROM *MILTON*, LINES 19–36

Thou perceivest the Flowers put forth their precious
Odours;
And none can tell how from so small a centre comes such
sweet,
Forgetting that within that centre Eternity expands
Its ever-during doors, that Og and Anak fiercely guard.
First, ere the morning breaks, joy opens in the flowery
bosoms,
Joy even to tears, which the Sun rising dries: first the
Wild Thyme
And Meadow-sweet, downy and soft, waving among the
reeds,
Light springing on the air, lead the sweet dance; they wake
The Honeysuckle sleeping on the oak; the flaunting beauty
Revels along upon the wind; the White-thorn, lovely May,
Opens her many lovely eyes; listening the Rose still sleeps –
None dare to wake her; soon she bursts her crimson –
curtain'd bed
And comes forth in the majesty of beauty. Every Flower,
The Pink, the Jessamine, the Wallflower, the Carnation,
The Jonquil, the mild Lily opes her heavens; every Tree
And Flower and Herb soon fill the air with an
innumerable dance,
Yet all in order sweet and lovely. Men are sick with love!
Such is the Vision of the lamentation of Beulah over
Ololon.

William Blake (1757–1827)

JUNE

Balmy-sweet Summer Twilight

Foxgloves

The foxglove bells, with lolling tongue,
Will not reveal what peals were rung
In Faery, in Faery,
A thousand ages gone.
All the golden clappers hang
As if but now the changes rang;
Only from the mottled throat
Never any echoes float.
Quite forgotten, in the wood,
Pale, crowded steeples rise;
All the time that they have stood
None has heard their melodies.
Deep, deep in wizardry
All the foxglove belfries stand.
Should they startle over the land,
None would know what bells they be.
Never any wind can ring them,
Nor the great black bees that swing them –
Every crimson bell, down-slanted,
Is so utterly enchanted.

Mary Webb (1881–1927)

Thyrsis

A MONODY, TO COMMEMORATE THE AUTHOR'S FRIEND, ARTHUR HUGH CLOUGH, WHO DIED AT FLORENCE, 1861

VERSES 6 AND 7

So, some tempestuous morn in early June,
When the year's primal burst of bloom is o'er,
Before the roses and the longest day –
When garden-walks and all the grassy floor
With blossoms red and white of fallen May
And chestnut-flowers are strewn –
So have I heard the cuckoo's parting cry,
From the wet field, through the vext garden-trees,
Come with the volleying rain and tossing breeze:
The bloom is gone, and with the bloom go I!

Too quick despairer, wherefore wilt thou go?
Soon will the high Midsummer pomps come on,
Soon will the musk carnations break and swell,
Soon shall we have gold-dusted snapdragon,
Sweet-William with his homely cottage-smell,
And stocks in fragrant blow;
Roses that down the alleys shine afar,
And open, jasmine-muffled lattices,
And groups under the dreaming garden-trees,
And the full moon, and the white evening-star.

Matthew Arnold (1822–1888)

The Nightingale and Glow-worm

LINES 1–26

A nightingale, that all day long
Had cheer'd the village with his song,
Nor yet at eve his note suspended,
Nor yet when eventide was ended,
Began to feel, as well he might,
The keen demands of appetite;
When, looking eagerly around,
He spied far off, upon the ground,
A something shining in the dark,
And knew the glow-worm by his spark;
So, stooping down from hawthorn top,
He thought to put him in his crop;
The worm, aware of his intent,
Harangued him thus right eloquent –
Did you admire my lamp, quoth he,
As much as I your minstrelsy,
You would abhor to do me wrong,
As much as I to spoil your song,
For 'twas the self-same pow'r divine
Taught you to sing, and me to shine,
That you with music, I with light,
Might beautify and cheer the night.
The songster heard his short oration,
And warbling out his approbation,
Releas'd him, as my story tells,
And found a supper somewhere else.

William Cowper (1731–1800)

Dusk in June

Evening, and all the birds
  In a chorus of shimmering sound
Are easing their hearts of joy
  For miles around.

The air is blue and sweet,
  The first few stars are white, –
Oh let me like the birds
  Sing before night.

Sara Teasdale (1884–1933)

Now Welcom Somer

FROM *THE PARLEMENT OF FOULES*, LINES 680–692

Now welcom somer, with thy sonne softe,
That hast this wintres weders over-shake,
And driven awey the longe nyghtes blake!

Saynt Valentyn, that art ful hy on-lofte; –
Thus singen smale foules for thy sake –
Now welcom somer, with thy sonne softe,
That hast this wintres weders over-shake.

Wel han they cause for to gladen ofte,
Sith ech of hem recovered hath his make;
Ful blisful may they singen whan they wake:
Now welcom somer, with thy sonne softe
That hast this wintres weders over-shake
And driven awey the longe nyghtes blake.

Geoffrey Chaucer (c.1343–1400)

6 JUNE

The Marigold

WHILST I THE SUN'S BRIGHT FACE MAY VIEW,
I WILL NO MEANER LIGHT PURSUE.
LINES 1–18

When with a serious musing I behold
The grateful and obsequious marigold;
How duly every morning, she displays
Her open breast when Titan spreads his rays;
How she observes him in his daily walk,
Still bending towards him her tender stalk;
How, when he down declines, she droops and mourns,
Bedewed (as 'twere) with tears, till he returns;
And how she vails her flow'rs when he is gone,
As if she scornèd to be lookèd on
By an inferior eye, or did contemn
To wait upon a meaner light than him.
When this I meditate, methinks the flowers
Have spirits far more generous than ours,
And give us fair examples to despise
The servile fawnings and idolatries
Wherewith we court these earthly things below,
Which merit not the service we bestow.

George Wither (1588–1667)

The Sea by Moonlight

Sleepless I lie
the long night through.

In the distance
the whispering of the sea,
in which we were
but this afternoon –
like two fishes.

No, the sea does not give up.
Her restless body moves,
even in the night,
while the clear-faced moon –
her lover –
sparkles in her belly,
and the land lies still in sleep.

David Austin (1926–2018)

To a Skylark

VERSES 1–7

Hail to thee, blithe Spirit!
    Bird thou never wert,
That from Heaven, or near it,
    Pourest thy full heart
In profuse strains of unpremeditated art.

Higher still and higher
    From the earth thou springest
Like a cloud of fire;
    The blue deep thou wingest,
And singing still dost soar, and soaring ever singest.

In the golden lightning
    Of the sunken sun,
O'er which clouds are bright'ning,
    Thou dost float and run;
Like an unbodied joy whose race is just begun.

The pale purple even
    Melts around thy flight;
Like a star of heaven
    In the broad daylight
Thou art unseen, but yet I hear thy shrill delight,

Keen as are the arrows
    Of that silver sphere,
Whose intense lamp narrows
    In the white dawn clear
Until we hardly see – we feel that it is there.

All the earth and air
    With thy voice is loud,
As, when night is bare,
    From one lonely cloud
The moon rains out her beams, and Heaven is overflowed.

What thou art we know not;
    What is most like thee?
From rainbow clouds there flow not
    Drops so bright to see
As from thy presence showers a rain of melody.

Percy Bysshe Shelley (1792–1822)

9 JUNE

Brightening Fields

FROM *SUMMER, THE SEASONS*

From brightening fields of ether fair disclosed,
Child of the sun, refulgent Summer comes,
In pride of youth, and felt through Nature's depth:
He comes attended by the sultry hours,
And ever-fanning breezes, on his way;
While, from his ardent look, the turning Spring
Averts her blushful face; and earth, and skies,
All-smiling, to his hot domain leaves.
  Hence, let me haste into the mid-wood shade,
Where scarce a sunbeam wanders through the gloom;
And on the dark-green grass, beside the brink
Of haunted stream, that by the roots of oak
Rolls o'er the rocky channel, lie at large,
And sing the glories of the circling year.

James Thomson (1700–1748)

A Summer Twilight

It is a Summer twilight, balmy-sweet,
A twilight brighten'd by an infant moon,
Fraught with the fairest light of middle June;
The lonely garden echoes to my feet,
And hark! O hear I not the gentle dews,
Fretting the silent forest in his sleep?
Or does the stir of housing insects creep
Thus faintly on mine ear? Day's many hues
Waned with the paling light and are no more,
And none but reptile pinions beat the air:
The bat is hunting softly by my door,
And, noiseless as the snow-flake, leaves his lair;
O'er the still copses flitting here and there,
Wheeling the self-same circuit o'er and o'er.

Charles Tennyson Turner (1808–1879)

The Voice of Nature

I stand on the cliff and watch the veiled sun paling
  A silver field afar in the mournful sea,
The scourge of the surf, and plaintive gulls sailing
  At ease on the gale that smites the shuddering lea:
      Whose smile severe and chaste
  June never hath stirred to vanity, nor age defaced.
In lofty thought strive, O spirit, for ever:
In courage and strength pursue thine own endeavour.

Ah! if it were only for thee, thou restless ocean
  Of waves that follow and roar, the sweep of the tides;
Wer't only for thee, impetuous wind, whose motion
  Precipitate all o'errides, and turns, nor abides:
      For you sad birds and fair,
  Or only for thee, bleak cliff, erect in the air;
Then well could I read wisdom in every feature,
O well should I understand the voice of Nature.

But far away, I think, in the Thames valley,
  The silent river glides by flowery banks:
And birds sing sweetly in branches that arch an alley
  Of cloistered trees, moss-grown in their ancient ranks:
      Where if a light air stray,
  'Tis laden with hum of bees and scent of may.
Love and peace be thine, O spirit, for ever:
Serve thy sweet desire: despise endeavour.

And if it were only for thee, entrancèd river,
  That scarce dost rock the lily on her airy stem,
Or stir a wave to murmur, or a rush to quiver;
  Wer't but for the woods, and summer asleep in them:
          For you my bowers green,
  My hedges of rose and woodbine, with walks between,
Then well could I read wisdom in every feature,
O well should I understand the voice of Nature.

Robert Bridges (1844–1930)

The Hills

Sometimes I think the hills
That loom across the harbor
Lie there like sleeping dragons,
Crouched one above another.
With trees for tufts of fur
Growing all up and down
The ridges and humps of their backs,
And orange cliffs for claws
Dipped in the sea below.
Sometimes a wisp of smoke
Rises out of the hollows,
As if in their dragon sleep
They dreamed of strange old battles.

What if the hills should stir
Some day and stretch themselves,
Shake off the clinging trees
And all the clustered houses?

Rachel Field (1894–1942)

13 JUNE

The Woods of Westermain

VERSE 1

Enter these enchanted woods,
  You who dare
Nothing harms beneath the leaves
More than waves a swimmer cleaves.
Toss your heart up with the lark,
Foot at pace with mouse and worm,
  Fair you fare.
Only at the dread of dark
Quaver, and they quit their form:
Thousand eyeballs under hoods
  Have you by the hair.
Enter these enchanted woods,
  You who dare.

George Meredith (1828–1909)

Renascence

LINES 1–26

All I could see from where I stood
Was three long mountains and a wood;
I turned and looked another way,
And saw three islands in a bay.
So with my eyes I traced the line
Of the horizon, thin and fine,
Straight around till I was come
Back to where I'd started from;
And all I saw from where I stood
Was three long mountains and a wood.
Over these things I could not see;
These were the things that bounded me;
And I could touch them with my hand,
Almost, I thought, from where I stand.
And all at once things seemed so small
My breath came short, and scarce at all.
But, sure, the sky is big, I said;
Miles and miles above my head;
So here upon my back I'll lie
And look my fill into the sky.
And so I looked, and, after all,
The sky was not so very tall.
The sky, I said, must somewhere stop,
And – sure enough! – I see the top!
The sky, I thought, is not so grand;
I 'most could touch it with my hand!

Edna St Vincent Millay (1892–1950)

Tree Dreaming

Last night I dreamt
a tree was dreaming
me
all night
I was trying
to decipher
I can't carry
its knowledge
into the waking
with me   instead
I reach always
over into the dream-t

but it did speak
to me it did   right there
I heard the language &
confirmed what I had known
I told this tree to keep on
coming   I'd grow
more receptive
to its language
so that I might
carry it out of
this vision
with me

Jason Allen-Paisant (1980–)

Dover Beach

The sea is calm to-night.
The tide is full, the moon lies fair
Upon the straits; – on the French coast the light
Gleams and is gone; the cliffs of England stand,
Glimmering and vast, out in the tranquil bay.
Come to the window, sweet is the night air!
Only, from the ling line of spray
Where the sea meets the moon-blanch'd land,
Listen! you hear the grating roar
Of pebbles which the waves draw back, and fling,
At their return, up the high strand,
Begin, and cease, and then again begin,
With tremulous cadence slow, and bring
The eternal note of sadness in.

Sophocles long ago
Heard it on the Ægæan, and it brought
Into his mind the turbid ebb and flow
Of human misery; we
Find also in the sound a thought,
Hearing it by this distant northern sea.

The Sea of Faith
Was once, at the full, and round earth's shore
Lay like the folds of a bright girdle furl'd.
But now I only hear
Its melancholy, long, withdrawing roar,
Retreating, to the breath
Of the night-wind, down the vast edges drear
And naked shingles of this world.

Ah, love, let us be true
To one another! for the world, which seems
To lie before us like a land of dreams,
So various, so beautiful, so new,
Hath really neither joy, nor love, nor light,
Nor certitude, nor peace, nor help for pain;
And we are here as on a darkling plain
Swept with confused alarms of struggle and flight,
Where ignorant armies clash by night.

Matthew Arnold (1822–1888)

The Lily and the Rose

The nymph must lose her female friend
 If more admir'd than she –
But where will fierce contention end
 If flow'rs can disagree?

Within the garden's peaceful scene
 Appear'd two lovely foes,
Aspiring to the rank of queen –
 The Lily and the Rose.

The Rose soon redden'd into rage,
 And, swelling with disdain,
Appeal'd to many a poet's page
 To prove her right to reign.

The Lily's height bespoke command –
 A fair imperial flow'r,
She seemed design'd for Flora's hand,
 The sceptre of her pow'r.

This civil bick'ring and debate
 The goddess chanc'd to hear,
And flew to save, ere yet too late,
 The pride of the parterre. –

Your's is, she said, the nobler hue,
  And your's the statelier mien,
And, till a third surpasses you,
  Let each be deem'd a queen.

Thus, sooth'd and reconcil'd, each seeks
  The fairest British fair,
The seat of empire is her cheeks,
  They reign united there.

William Cowper (1731–1800)

A Waterpiece

The wild-rose bush lets loll
Her sweet-breathed petals on the pearl-smoothed pool,
The bream-pool overshadowed with the cool
Of oaks where myriad mumbling wings patrol.
There the live dimness burrs with droning glees
Of hobby-horses with their starting eyes
And violet humble-bees and dizzy flies;
That from the dewsprings drink the honeyed lees.

Up the slow stream the immemorial bream
(For when had Death dominion over them?)
Through green pavilions of ghost leaf and stem,
A conclave of blue shadows in a dream,
Glide on; idola that forgotten plan,
Incomparably wise, the doom of man.

Edmund Blunden (1896–1974)

Moonrise, June 19

I awoke in the midsummer not-to-call night, | in the white and
the walk of the morning:
The móon, dwíndled and thínned to the fringe | of a fingernail
héld to the cándle,
Or páring of páradisáïcal frúit, | lóvely in wáning but lústreless,
Stepped from the stool, drew back from the barrow, | of dark
Maenefa the mountain;
A cusp still clasped him, a fluke yet fanged him, | entangled
him, not quit utterly.
This was the prized, the desirable sight, | unsought, presented
so easily,
Parted me leaf and leaf, divided me, | eyelid and eyelid of
slumber.

Gerard Manley Hopkins (1844–1889)

Adlestrop

Yes. I remember Adlestrop –
The name, because one afternoon
Of heat the express-train drew up there
Unwontedly. It was late June.

The steam hissed. Someone cleared his throat.
No one left and no one came
On the bare platform. What I saw
Was Adlestrop – only the name

And willows, willow-herb, and grass,
And meadowsweet, and haycocks dry,
No whit less still and lonely fair
Than the high cloudlets in the sky.

And for that minute a blackbird sang
Close by, and round him, mistier,
Farther and farther, all the birds
Of Oxfordshire and Gloucestershire.

Edward Thomas (1878–1917)

Endymion

BOOK I, LINES 1–33

A thing of beauty is a joy for ever:
Its loveliness increases; it will never
Pass into nothingness; but will still keep
A bower quiet for us, and a sleep
Full of sweet dreams, and health, and quiet breathing.
Therefore, on every morrow, we are wreathing
A flowery band to bind us to the earth,
Spite of despondence, of the inhuman dearth
Of noble natures, of the gloomy days,
Of all the unhealthy and o'er-darkened ways
Made for our searching: yes, in spite of all,
Some shape of beauty moves away the pall
From our dark spirits. Such the sun, the moon,
Trees old, and young, sprouting a shady boon
For simple sheep; and such are daffodils
With the green world they live in; and clear rills
That for themselves a cooling covert make
'Gainst the hot season; the mid forest brake,
Rich with a sprinkling of fair musk-rose blooms:
And such too is the grandeur of the dooms
We have imagined for the mighty dead;

All lovely tales that we have heard or read:
An endless fountain of immortal drink,
Pouring unto us from heaven's brink.

Nor do we merely feel these essences
For one short hour; no, even as the trees
That whisper round a temple become soon
Dear as the temple's self, so does the moon,
The passion poesy, glories infinite,
Haunt us till they become a cheering light
Unto our souls and bound to us so fast,
That, whether there be shine, or gloom o'ercast,
They always must be with us, or we die.

John Keats (1795–1821)

The Sundew

A little marsh-plant, yellow green,
And pricked at lip with tender red.
Tread close, and either way you tread
Some faint black water jets between
Lest you should bruise the curious head.

A live thing maybe; who shall know?
The summer knows and suffers it;
For the cool moss is thick and sweet
Each side, and saves the blossom so
That it lives out the long June heat.

The deep scent of the heather burns
About it; breathless though it be,
Bow down and worship; more than we
Is the least flower whose life returns,
Least weed renascent in the sea.

We are vexed and cumbered in earth's sight
With wants, with many memories;
These see their mother what she is,
Glad-growing, till August leave more bright
The apple-coloured cranberries.

Wind blows and bleaches the strong grass,
Blown all one way to shelter it
From trample of strayed kine, with feet
Felt heavier than the moorhen was,
Strayed up past patches of wild wheat.

You call it sundew: how it grows,
If with its colour it have breath,
If life taste sweet to it, if death
Pain its soft petal, no man knows:
Man has no sight or sense that saith.

My sundew, grown of gentle days,
In these green miles the spring begun
Thy growth ere April had half done
With the soft secret of her ways
Or June made ready for the sun.

O red-lipped mouth of marsh-flower,
I have a secret halved with thee.
The name that is love's name to me
Thou knowest, and the face of her
Who is my festival to see.

The hard sun, as thy petals knew,
Coloured the heavy moss-water:
Thou wert not worth green midsummer
Nor fit to live to August blue,
O sundew, not remembering her.

Algernon Charles Swinburne (1837–1909)

Night

FROM *SONGS OF INNOCENCE*, VERSES 1 AND 2

The sun descending in the west,
The evening star does shine;
The birds are silent in their nest.
And I must seek for mine.
The moon, like a flower
In heaven's high bower,
With silent delight
Sits and smiles on the night.

Farewell, green fields and happy groves,
Where flocks have took delight:
Where lambs have nibbled, silent moves
The feet of angels bright;
Unseen they pour blessing,
And joy without ceasing,
On each bud and blossom,
And each sleeping bosom.

William Blake (1757–1827)

Sonnet 98

From you have I been absent in the spring,
When proud-pied April, dressed in all his trim,
Hath put a spirit of youth in everything,
That heavy Saturn laughed and leaped with him,
Yet nor the lays of birds, nor the sweet smell
Of different flowers in odor and in hue,
Could make me any summer's story tell,
Or from their proud lap pluck them where they grew.
Nor did I wonder at the lily's white,
Nor praise the deep vermilion in the rose;
They were but sweet, but figures of delight,
Drawn after you, you pattern of all those.
Yet seemed it winter still, and, you away,
As with your shadow I with these did play.

William Shakespeare (1564–1616)

A Boar Buys Real Estate in Fukushima Prefecture

for a snootful of roots, fallen fruits, and the carrion
of a cream-coloured marten. She scuffs a four
-hoofed footpath into the linoleum. Enough room
for her furs. The tusks of past lovers. Her life
without leaving at sunrise—she can already see it.
Her birthplace was razed for a house like this.
Market's recovering, the boar realtor says. Scrap
and build. This world is cursed but you find reasons
to keep on living. The boar is quiet. She is happy. She
has survived on this land for a decade. For the young
everything needs fixing. From her window
she can see the mountains, just like
from any window.

Shastra Deo

The Fields of Dark

The wreathing vine within the porch
  Is in the heart of me,
The roses that the noondays scorch
  Burn on in memory;
Alone at night I quench the light,
  And without star or spark
The grass and trees press to my knees,
  And flowers throng the dark.

The leaves that loose their hold at noon
  Drop on my face like rain,
And in the watches of the moon
  I feel them fall again.
By day I stray how far away
  To stream and wood and steep,
But on my track they all come back
  To haunt the vale of sleep.

The fields of light are clover-brimmed,
  Or grassed or daisy-starred;
The fields of dark are softly dimmed,
  And safety twilight-barred;
But in the gloom that fills my room
  I cannot fail to mark
The grass and trees about my knees,
  The flowers in the dark.

Ethelwyn Wetherald (1857–1940)

The Vision of Sir Launfal

PRELUDE TO THE PART FIRST, LINES 33–56

And what is so rare as a day in June?
  Then, if ever, come perfect days;
Then Heaven tries earth if it be in tune,
  And over it softly her warm ear lays:
Whether we look, or whether we listen,
We hear life murmur, or see it glisten;
Every clod feels a stir of might,
  An instinct within it that reaches and towers,
And, groping blindly above it for light,
  Climbs to a soul in grass and flowers;
The flush of life may well be seen
  Thrilling back over hills and valleys;
The cowslip startles in meadows green,
  The buttercup catches the sun in its chalice,
And there's never a leaf nor a blade too mean
  To be some happy creature's palace;
The little bird sits at his door in the sun,
  Atilt like a blossom among the leaves,
And lets his illumined being o'errun
  With the deluge of summer it receives;
His mate feels the eggs beneath her wings,
And the heart in her dumb breast flutters and sings;
He sings to the wide world, and she to her nest, –
In the nice ear of Nature which song is the best?

James Russell Lowell (1819–1891)

I Love Flowers

SIBYLLA FROM *DEATH'S JEST-BOOK*, ACT V, SCENE III

I love flowers too; not for a young girl's reason,
But because these brief visitors to us
Rise yearly from the neighbourhood of the dead,
To show us how far fairer and more lovely
Their world is; and return thither again,
Like parting friends that beckon us to follow,
And lead the way silent and smilingly.
Fair is the season when they come to us,
Unfolding the delights of that existence
Which is below us: 'tis the time of spirits,
Who with the flowers, and, like them, leave their graves:
But when the earth is sealed, and none dare come
Upwards to cheer us, and man's left alone,
We have cold, cutting winter.

Thomas Lovell Beddoes (1803–1849)

To the Grasshopper and the Cricket

Green little vaulter in the sunny grass,
Catching your heart up at the feel of June,
Sole voice that's heard amidst the lazy noon,
When even the bees lag at the summoning brass,
And you, warm little housekeeper, who class
With those who think the candles come too soon,
Loving the fire, and with your tricksome tune
Nick the glad silent moments as they pass;
Oh sweet and tiny cousins, that belong
One to the fields, the other to the hearth,
Both have your sunshine; both, though small, are strong
At your clear hearts; and both were sent on earth
To sing in thoughtful ears this natural song –
Indoors and out, summer and winter, Mirth.

Leigh Hunt (1784–1859)

Summer

Winter is cold-hearted,
        Spring is yea and nay,
Autumn is a weathercock
        Blown every way:
Summer days for me
        When every leaf is on its tree;

When Robin's not a beggar,
        And Jenny Wren's a bride,
And larks hang singing, singing, singing,
        Over the wheat-fields wide,

And anchored lilies ride,
        And the pendulum spider

Swings from side to side;

And blue-black beetles transact business,
        And gnats fly in a host,
And furry caterpillars hasten
        That no time be lost,
And moths grow fat and thrive,
        And ladybirds arrive.

Before green apples blush,
        Before green nuts embrown,
Why, one day in the country
        Is worth a month in town;
        Is worth a day and a year
Of the dusty, musty, lag-last fashion
        That days drone elsewhere.

Christina Rossetti (1830–1894)

JULY

Each Daisy Stands Like a Star

1 JULY

The Thistle's Grown aboon the Rose

VERSE 1

Full white the Bourbon lily blows,
And farer haughty England's rose.
Nor shall unsung the symbol smile,
Green Ireland, of thy lovely isle.
In Scotland grows a warlike flower,
Too rough to bloom in lady's bower;
His crest. when high the soldier bears,
And spurs his courser on the spears.
O, there it blossoms – there it blows –
The thistle's grown aboon the rose.

Alan Cunningham (1784–1842)

The Brook

Seated once by a brook, watching a child
Chiefly that paddled, I was thus beguiled.
Mellow the blackbird sang and sharp the thrush
Not far off in the oak and hazel brush,
Unseen. There was a scent like honeycomb
From mugwort dull. And down upon the dome
Of the stone the cart-horse kicks against so oft
A butterfly alighted. From aloft
He took the heat of the sun, and from below.
On the hot stone he perched contented so,
As if never a cart would pass again
That way; as if I were the last of men
And he the first of insects to have earth
And sun together and to know their worth.
I was divided between him and the gleam,
The motion, and the voices, of the stream,
The waters running frizzled over gravel,
That never vanish and for ever travel.
A grey flycatcher silent on a fence
And I sat as if we had been there since
The horseman and the horse lying beneath
The fir-tree-covered barrow on the heath,
The horseman and the horse with silver shoes,
Galloped the downs last. All that I could lose
I lost. And then the child's voice raised the dead.
'No one's been here before' was what she said
And what I felt, yet never should have found
A word for, while I gathered sight and sound.

Edward Thomas (1878–1917)

Twilight-Piece

The golden river-reach afar
  Kisses the golden skies of even,
And there's the first faint lover's star
  Alight along the walls of heaven.

The river murmurs to the boughs,
  The boughs make music each to each,
And still an amorous west wind soughs
  And loiters down the lonesome reach.

And here on the slim arch that spans
  The rippling stream, in dark outline,
You see the poor old fisherman's
  Bowed form and patient rod and line.

A picture better than all art,
  Since none could catch that sunset stain,
Or set in the soft twilight's heart
  This small strange touch of human pain!

Victor Plarr (1863–1929)

Wild Honeysuckle

Fair flower, that dost so comely grow,
Hid in this silent, dull retreat,
Untouched thy honied blossoms blow,
Unseen thy little branches greet:
  No roving foot shall crush thee here,
  No busy hand provoke a tear.

By Nature's self in white arrayed,
She bade thee shun the vulgar eye,
And planted here the guardian shade,
And sent soft waters murmuring by;
  Thus quietly thy summer goes,
  Thy days declining to repose.

Smit with those charms, that must decay,
I grieve to see your future doom;
They died – nor were those flowers more gay,
The flowers that did in Eden bloom;
  Unpitying frosts and Autumn's power
  Shall leave no vestige of this flower.

From morning suns and evening dews
At first thy little being came;
If nothing once, you nothing lose,
For when you die you are the same;
  The space between is but an hour,
  The frail duration of flower.

Philip Freneau (1752–1832)

Ocean, an Ode

VERSES 1 AND 2

Sweet rural scene!
Of flocks and green!
At careless ease my limbs are spread;
All nature still
But yonder rill;
And listening pines not o'er my head:

In prospect wide,
The boundless tide!
Waves cease to foam, and winds to roar;
Without a breeze,
The curling seas
Dance on, in measure, to the shore.

Edward Young (1683–1765)

Dawn Revisited

Imagine you wake up
with a second chance: The blue jay
hawks his pretty wares
and the oak still stands, spreading
glorious shade. If you don't look back,

the future never happens.
How good to rise in sunlight,
in the prodigal smell of biscuits -
eggs and sausage on the grill.
The whole sky is yours

to write on, blown open
to a blank page. Come on,
shake a leg! You'll never know
who's down there, frying those eggs,
if you don't get up and see.

Rita Dove (1952–)

A Bird Came Down the Walk

A Bird came down the Walk –
He did not know I saw –
He bit an Angleworm in halves
And ate the fellow, raw,

And then, he drank a Dew
From a convenient Grass –
And then hopped sidewise to the Wall
To let a Beetle pass –

He glanced with rapid eyes,
That hurried all abroad –
They looked like frightened Beads, I thought,
He stirred his Velvet Head

Like one in danger, Cautious,
I offered him a Crumb,
And he unrolled his feathers,
And rowed him softer Home –

Than Oars divide the Ocean,
Too silver for a seam,
Or Butterflies, off Banks of Noon,
Leap, plashless as they swim.

Emily Dickinson (1830–1886)

Evening Rain

What is lovelier than rain that lingers
Falling through the western light?
The light that's red between my fingers
Bathes infinite heaven's remotest height.

Whither will the cloud its darkness carry
Whose trembling drops about me spill?
Two worlds, of shadow and splendour, marry:
I stand between them rapt and still.

Laurence Binyon (1869–1943)

9 JULY

The Glow-Worm

TRANSLATED BY WILLIAM COWPER

VERSES 1–5

Beneath the hedge or near the stream,
A worm is known to stray,
That shows by night a lucid beam,
Which disappears by day.

Disputes have been and still prevail
From whence his rays proceed;
Some give that honour to his tail,
And others to his head.

But this is sure, – the hand of might
That kindles up the skies,
Gives *him* a modicum of light,
Proportion'd to his size.

Perhaps indulgent nature meant
By such a lamp bestow'd,
To bid the trav'ler, as he went,
Be careful where he trod;

Nor crush a worm, whose useful light
Might serve, however small,
To show a stumbling stone by night,
And save him from a fall.

Vincent Bourne (1695–1747)

Sonnet to the River Otter

Dear native Brook! wild Streamlet of the West!
  How many various-fated years have past,
  What happy and what mournful hours, since last
I skimm'd the smooth thin stone along thy breast,
Numbering its light leaps! yet so deep imprest
Sink the sweet scenes of childhood, that mine eyes
  I never shut amid the sunny ray,
But straight with all their tints thy waters rise,
  Thy crossing plank, thy marge with willows grey,
And bedded sand that, vein'd with various dyes
Gleam'd through thy bright transparence! On my way,
  Visions of Childhood! oft have ye beguil'd
Lone manhood's cares, yet waking fondest sighs:
  Ah! that once more I were a careless Child!

Samuel Taylor Coleridge (1772–1834)

The World Below the Brine

The world below the brine,
Forests at the bottom of the sea, the branches and leaves,
Sea-lettuce, vast lichens, strange flowers and seeds, the
thick tangle, openings, and pink turf,
Different colors, pale gray and green, purple, white, and
gold, the play of light through the water,
Dumb swimmers there among the rocks, coral, gluten,
grass, rushes, and the aliment of the swimmers,
Sluggish existences grazing there suspended, or slowly
crawling close to the bottom,
The sperm-whale at the surface blowing air and spray, or
disporting with his flukes,
The leaden-eyed shark, the walrus, the turtle, the hairy
sea-leopard, and the sting-ray,
Passions there, wars, pursuits, tribes, sight in those ocean
-depths, breathing that thick-breathing air, as so many do,
The change thence to the sight here, and to the subtle air
breathed by beings like us who walk this sphere,
The change onward from ours to that of beings who walk
other spheres.

Walt Whitman (1819–1892)

Epithalamion

LINES 1–13

Hark, hearer, hear what I do; lend a thought now, make believe
We are leaf-whelmed somewhere with the hood
Of some branchy bunchy bushybowered wood,
Southern dene or Lancashire clough or Devon cleave,
That leans along the loins of hills, where a candycoloured, where a gluegold-brown
Marbled river, boisterously beautiful, between
Roots and rocks is danced and dandled, all in froth and waterblowballs, down.
We are there, when we hear a shout
That the hanging honeysuck, the dogeared hazels in the cover
Makes dither, makes hover
And the riot of a rout
Of, it must be, boys from the town
Bathing: it is summer's sovereign good.

Gerard Manley Hopkins (1844–1889)

Flower in the Crannied Wall

Flower in the crannied wall,
I pluck you out of the crannies,
I hold you here, root and all, in my hand,
Little flower – but if I could understand
What you are, root and all, all in all,
I should know what God and man is.

Alfred, Lord Tennyson (1809–1892)

14 JULY

You Spotted Snakes with Double Tongue

FROM *A MIDSUMMER NIGHT'S DREAM*, ACT II, SCENE II

You spotted snakes with double tongue,
  Thorny hedgehogs, be not seen;
Newts and blind-worms, do no wrong;
  Come not near our Fairy Queen.

  Philomel, with melody,
  Sing in our sweet lullaby;
Lulla, lulla, lullaby; lulla, lulla, lullaby!
      Never harm
      Nor spell nor charm
    Come our lovely lady nigh
    So good night, with lullaby.

Weaving spiders, come not here;
  Hence, you long-legged spinners, hence;
Beetles black, approach not near;
  Worm nor snail do no offence.

  Philomel, with melody,
  Sing in our sweet lullaby;
Lulla, lulla, lullaby; lulla, lulla, lullaby!
      Never harm
      Nor spell nor charm
    Come our lovely lady nigh
    So good night, with lullaby.

William Shakespeare (1564–1616)

The Rainy Summer

There's much afoot in heaven and earth this year;
The winds hunt up the sun, hunt up the moon,
Trouble the dubious dawn, hasten the drear
Height of a threatening noon.

No breath of boughs, no breath of leaves, of fronds,
May linger or grow warm; the trees are loud;
The forest, rooted, tosses in her bonds,
And strains against the cloud.

No scents may pause within the garden-fold;
The rifled flowers are cold as ocean-shells;
Bees, humming in the storm, carry their cold
Wild honey to cold cells.

Alice Meynell (1847–1922)

Nocturne

Day, like a flower of gold fades on its crimson bed;
For the many chambered night unbars to shut its
  sweetness up;
From earth and heaven fast drawn together a heavy
  stillness is shed,
And our hearts drink the shadowy splendour from a
  brimming cup.

For the indrawn breath of beauty thrills the holy caves
  of night;
Shimmering winds of heaven fall gently and mysterious
  hands caress
Our wan brows with cooling rapture of the delicate
  starlight
Dropping from the night's blue walls in endless veils of
  loveliness.

Isaac Rosenberg (1890–1918)

Little Birds of the Night

Little birds of the night
Aye, they have much to tell
Perching there in rows
Blinking at me with their serious eyes
Recounting of flowers they have seen and loved
Of meadows and groves of the distance
And pale sands at the foot of the sea
And breezes that fly in the leaves.
They are vast in experience
These little birds that come in the night.

Stephen Crane (1871–1900)

18 JULY

A Cat's Conscience

A dog will often steal a bone,
But conscience lets him not alone,
And by his tail his guilt is known.

But cats consider theft a game,
And, howsoever you may blame,
Refuse the slightest sign of shame.

When food mysteriously goes,
The chances are that Pussy knows
More than she leads you to suppose.

And hence there is no need for you,
If Puss declines a meal or to,
To feel her pulse and make ado.

Anon

Deer

Shy in their herding dwell the fallow deer.
They are spirits of wild sense. Nobody near
Comes upon their pastures. There a life they live,
Of sufficient beauty, phantom, fugitive,
Treading as in jungles free leopards do,
Printless as evelight, instant as dew.
The great kine are patient, and home-coming sheep
Know our bidding. The fallow deer keep
Delicate and far their counsels wild,
Never to be folded reconciled
To the spoiling hand as the poor flocks are;
Lightfoot, and swift, and unfamiliar,
These you may not hinder, unconfined
Beautiful flocks of the mind.

John Drinkwater (1882–1937)

At Night

The wind is singing through the trees to-night,
  A deep-voiced song of rushing cadences
  And crashing intervals. No summer breeze
Is this, though hot July is at its height,
Gone is her gentler music; with delight
  She listens to this booming like the seas,
  These elemental, loud necessities
Which call to her to answer their swift might.
  Above the tossing trees shines down a star,
  Quietly bright; this wild, tumultuous joy
Quickens nor dims its splendour. And my mind,
  O Star! is filled with your white light, from far,
  So suffer me this one night to enjoy
The freedom of the onward sweeping wind.

Amy Lowell (1874–1925)

On a Drop of Dew

LINES 1–18

See how the Orient Dew,
  Shed from the Bosom of the Morn
  Into the blowing Roses,
Yet careless of its Mansion new
For the clear Region where 'twas born,
  Round in its self incloses:
  And in its little Globes Extent,
Frames as it can its native Element.
  How it the purple flow'r does slight,
    Scarce touching where it lyes,
  But gazing back upon the Skies,
    Shines with a mournful Light,
      Like its own Tear,
Because so long divided from the Sphear.
  Restless it roules and unsecure,
    Trembling lest it grow impure,
  Till the warm Sun pitty it's Pain,
And to the Skies exhale it back again.

Andrew Marvell (1621–1678)

22 JULY

The River God's Song

FROM *THE FAITHFUL SHEPHERDESS*

Do not fear to put thy feet
Naked in the river, sweet
Think not leach or newt or toad
Will bite thy foot when thou hast trod;
Nor let the water rising high,
As thou wadest in, make thee cry
And sob; but ever live with me,
And not a wave shall trouble thee.

John Fletcher (1579–1625)

Trees in the Garden

Ah in the thunder air
how still the trees are!

And the lime-tree, lovely and tall, every leaf silent
hardly looses even a last breath of perfume.

And the ghostly, creamy coloured little tree of leaves
white, ivory white among the rambling greens
how evanescent, variegated elder, she hesitates on the
green grass as if, in another moment, she would disappear
with all her grace of foam!

And the larch that is only a column, it goes up too tall
  to see:
and the balsam-pines that are blue with the grey-blue
  blueness of things from the sea,
and the young copper beech, its leaves red-rosey at the ends
how still they are together, they stand so still
in the thunder air, all strangers to one another
as the green grass glows upwards, strangers in the garden.

D. H. Lawrence (1885–1930)

24 JULY

The Woodpecker

I once a King and chief
Now am the tree-bark's thief,
Ever 'twixt trunk and leaf
Chasing the prey.

William Morris (1834–1896)

Among the Firs

And what a charm is in the rich hot scent
  Of old fir forests heated by the sun,
  Where drops of resin down the rough bark run,
And needle litter breathes its wonderment.

The old fir forests heated by the sun,
  Their thought shall linger like the lingering scent,
  Their beauty haunt us, and a wonderment
Of moss, of fern, of cones, of rills that run.

The needle litter breathes a wonderment;
  The crimson crans are sparkling in the sun;
  From tree to tree the scampering squirrels run;
The hum of insects blends with heat and scent.

The drops of resin down the rough bark run;
  And riper, ever riper, grows the scent;
  But eve has come, to end the wonderment,
And slowly up the tree trunk climbs the sun.

Eugene Lee-Hamilton (1845–1907)

The Grasshopper

VERSES 1–3

O thou that swingst upon the waving hair
  Of some well-fillèd oaten beard,
Drunk every night with a delicious tear
  Dropped thee from heaven, where now th' art reared;

The joys of earth and air are thine entire,
  That with thy feet and wings dost hop and fly;
And when thy poppy works thou dost retire
  To thy carved acorn bed to lie.

Up with the day, the sun thou welcom'st then,
  Sportst in the gilt plats of his beams,
And all these merry days mak'st merry men,
  Thyself, and melancholy streams.

Richard Lovelace (1618–1657)

The Bothie of Tober-Na-Vuolich

PART III, LINES 19–46

There is a stream, I name not its name, lest inquisitive tourist
Hunt it, and make it a lion, and get it at last into guide-books,
Springing far off from a loch unexplored in the folds of great mountains,
Falling two miles through rowan and stunted alder, enveloped
Then for four more in a forest of pine, where broad and ample
Spreads, to convey it, the glen with heathery slopes on both sides:
Broad and fair the stream, with occasional falls and narrows;
But, where the glen of its course approaches the vale of the river,
Met and blocked by a huge interposing mass of granite,
Scarce by a channel deep-cut, raging up, and raging onward,
Forces its flood through a passage so narrow a lady would step it.
There, across the great rocky wharves, a wooden bridge goes,
Carrying a path to the forest; below, three hundred yards, say,
Lower in level some twenty-five feet, through flats of shingle,
Stepping-stones and a cart-track cross in the open valley.

But in the interval here the boiling, pent-up water
Frees itself by a final descent, attaining a bason,
Ten feet wide and eighteen long, with whiteness and fury
Occupied partly, but mostly pellucid, pure, a mirror;
Beautiful there for the colour derived from green rocks
  under;
Beautiful, most of all, where beads of foam uprising
Mingle their clouds of white with the delicate hue of the
  stillness.
Cliff over cliff for its sides, with rowan and pendent birch
  boughs,
Here it lies, unthought of above at the bridge and pathway,
Still more enclosed from below by wood and rocky
  projection.
You are shut in, left alone with yourself and perfection of
  water,
Hid on all sides, left alone with yourself and the goddess
  of bathing.

Arthur Hugh Clough (1819–1861)

The Hairy Dog

My dog's so furry I've not seen
His face for years and years;
His eyes are buried out of sight,
I only guess his ears.

When people ask me for his breed,
I do not know or care;
He has the beauty of them all
Hidden beneath his hair.

Herbert Asquith (1881–1947)

Where Innocent Bright-eyed Daisies Are

Where innocent bright-eyed daisies are,
  With blades of grass between,
Each daisy stands up like a star
  Out of a sky of green.

Christina Rossetti (1830–1894)

Impressions II

LA FUITE DE LA LUNE

To outer senses there is peace,
A dreamy peace on either hand,
Deep silence in the shadowy land,
Deep silence where the shadows cease.

Save for a cry that echoes shrill
From some lone bird disconsolate;
A corncrake calling to its mate;
The answer from the misty hill.

An suddenly the moon withdraws
Her sickle from the lightening skies,
And to her sombre cavern flies,
Wrapped in a veil of yellow gauze.

Oscar Wilde (1854–1900)

Haze

Woof of the sun, ethereal gauze,
Woven of Nature's richest stuffs,
Visible heat, air-water, and dry sea,
Last conquest of the eye;
Toil of the day displayed, sun-dust,
Aerial surf upon the shores of earth,
Ethereal estuary, frith of light,
Breakers of air, billows of heat,
Fine summer spray on inland seas;
Bird of the sun, transparent-winged,
Owlet of noon, soft-pinioned,
From heath or stubble rising without song;
Establish thy serenity o'er the fields.

Henry David Thoreau (1817–1862)

AUGUST

Now Fades the Glimmering Landscape

Sounds in the Wood

Trees breathe
Quiet in the wood.
Winds hush
Cradled in the branches.
Jays squall
Carping in the startled tree-tops.
Tits pipe
Keen in the secret, the secret thicket.

Mavis Pilbeam (1946–)

A Hymn to the Evening

Soon as the sun forsook the eastern main
The pealing thunder shook the heav'nly plain;
Majestic grandeur! From the zephyr's wing,
Exhales the incense of the blooming spring.
Soft purl the streams, the birds renew their notes,
And through the air their mingled music floats.
Through all the heav'ns what beauteous dies are spread!
But the west glories in the deepest red:
So may our breasts with ev'ry virtue glow,
The living temples of our God below!
Fill'd with the praise of him who gives the light,
And draws the sable curtains of the night,
Let placid slumbers sooth each weary mind,
At morn to wake more heav'nly, more refin'd;
So shall the labours of the day begin
More pure, more guarded from the snares of sin.
Night's leaden sceptre seals my drowsy eyes,
Then cease, my song, till fair Aurora rise.

Phillis Wheatley (c. 1753–1784)

Summer Rain

Thick lay the dust, uncomfortably white,
In glaring mimicry of Arab sands.
The woods and mountains slept in hazy light;
The meadows look'd athirst and tawny tann'd;
The little rills had left their channels bare.
With scarce a pool to witness what they were;
And the shrunk river gleam'd 'mid oozy stones.
That stared like any famish'd giant's bones.

Sudden the hills grew black, and hot as stove
The air beneath; it was a toil to be.
There was a growling as of angry Jove,
Provoked by Juno's prying jealousy –
A flash – a crash – the firmament was split.
And down it came in drops – the smallest fit
To drown a bee in fox-glove bell conceal'd;
Joy fill'd the brook, and comfort cheer'd the field.

Hartley Coleridge (1796–1849)

No Matter

water laps grindingly dark on a lip
of teeming sand (worms/lost coins) &
those gathered (bodies weighted by
sleep) have little need for the torrent of
stars or the names of planets: limbs
containing bones at rest.

Joel Knight (1975–)

On Craig Ddu

FROM *INTERMEZZO: PASTORAL*

The sky through the leaves of the bracken,
Tenderly, pallidly blue,
Nothing but sky as I lie on the mountain-top.
Hark! for the wind as it blew,

Rustling the tufts of my bracken above me,
Brought from below
Into the silence the sound of the water.
Hark! for the oxen low,

Sheep are bleating, a dog
Barks, at a farm in the vale:
Blue, through the bracken, softly enveloping
Silence, a veil.

Arthur Symons (1865–1945)

The Rose

O Rose, thou art the flower of flowers, thou fragrant wonder,
Who shall describe thee in they ruddy prime,
Thy perfect fulness in the summer time,
When the pale leaves blushingly part asunder
And show the warm red heart lies glowing under?
Thou shouldst bloom surely in some sunny clime,
Untouched by blights and chilly Winter's rime,
Where lightnings never flash nor peals the thunder.
And yet in happier spheres they cannot need thee
So much as we do with our weight of woe;
Perhaps they would not tend, perhaps not heed thee,
And thou wouldst lonely and neglected grow;
And He Who is All-Wise, He hath decreed thee
To gladden earth and cheer all hearts below.

Christina Rossetti (1830–1894)

In the Water

FROM *A MIDSUMMER HOLIDAY*, VERSE 1

The sea is awake, and the sound of the song
  of the joy of her waking is rolled
From afar to the star that recedes, from anear
  to the wastes of the wild wide shore.
Her call is a trumpet compelling us homeward:
  if dawn in her east be acold,
From the sea shall we crave not her grace to rekindle
  the life that it kindled before,
Her breath to requicken, her bosom to rock us,
  her kisses to bless as of yore?
For the wind, with his wings half open, at pause
  in the sky, neither fettered nor free,
Leans waveward and flutters the ripple to laughter
  and fain would the twain of us be
Where lightly the wave yearns forward from under
  the curve of the deep dawn's dome,
And, full of the morning and fired with the pride
  of the glory thereof and the glee,
Strike out from the shore as the heart in us bids
  and beseeches, athirst for the foam.

Algernon Charles Swinburne (1837–1909)

Kingfisher

Dropping
Like a splinter from the sky
It knives the water,
Swiftly strikes,
Turns, surges
Up through the splattering surface,
Back to the willow branch,
Where it sits triumphant,
Wet feathers glistening,
Its silver catch
Dangling from its beak.

John Foster (1941–)

Ah! Sun-Flower

FROM *SONGS OF EXPERIENCE*

Ah, Sun-flower! weary of time,
Who countest the steps of the sun,
Seeking after that sweet golden clime
Where the traveller's journey is done.

Where the Youth pined away with desire,
And the pale Virgin shrouded in snow:
Arise from their graves, and aspire,
Where my Sun-flower wishes to go.

William Blake (1757–1827)

The Ousel Cock

FROM *A MIDSUMMER'S NIGHT DREAM,* ACT III, SCENE I

The ousel cock, so black of hue,
  With orange-tawny bill;
The throstle with his note so true,
  The wren with little quill.

The finch, the sparrow, and the lark,
  The plainsong cuckoo grey,
Whose note full many a man doth mark,
  And dares not answer 'Nay'

William Shakespeare (1564–1616)

The Estuary

A light elegant wall waves down
The riverside, for tidiness
Or decoration – this water
Needs little keeping in – but turns
The corner to face the ocean
And thickens to a bastion.

No one can really taste or smell
Where the salt starts but at one point
The first building looks out to sea
And the two sides of the river
Are forced apart by cold light
And wind and different grasses.

I see this now, but at one time
I had to believe that the two
Sides were almost identical.
I was a child who dared not seem
Gloomy. Traversing grey water
From the east side where I was born

And had spent a normal cross life,
To live gratefully with strangers
On the west side, I grinned and clowned.
I did not go back for ages
And became known for cheerfulness
In a house where all was not well.

Grief was a poltergeist that would
Not materialize but broke
Everything. Neither believed in
Nor dreaded, it took one decade
To appear, one to be recognized,
Then cleared the air wonderfully

So that nowadays I am able
To see the estuary as two
Distinct pieces of countryside,
Not a great deal to choose between
Them perhaps but at least different,
Rising normally from two roots.

On one bank, stiff fields of corn grow
To the hilltop, are draped over
It surrealistically.
On the other, little white boats
Sag sideways twice every day
As the sea pulls away their prop.

Patricia Beer (1919–1999)

Drawing Near the Light

Lo, when we wade the tangled wood,
In haste and hurry to be there,
Nought seem its leaves and blossoms good,
For all that they be fashioned fair.

But looking up, at last we see
The glimmer of the open light,
From o'er the place where we would be:
Then grow the very brambles bright.

So now, amidst our day of strife,
With many a matter glad we play,
When once we see the light of life
Gleam through the tangle of to-day.

William Morris (1834–1896)

Elegy Written in a Country Churchyard

VERSES 1–9

The curfew tolls the knell of parting day,
The lowing herd wind slowly o'er the lea,
The plowman homeward plods his weary way,
And leaves the world to darkness and to me.

Now fades the glimmering landscape on the sight,
And all the air a solemn stillness holds,
Save where the beetle wheels his droning flight,
And drowsy tinklings lull the distant folds;

Save that from yonder ivy-mantled tow'r
The mopeing owl does to the moon complain
Of such, as wand'ring near her secret bow'r,
Molest her ancient solitary reign.

Beneath those rugged elms, that yew-tree's shade,
Where heaves the turf in many a mould'ring heap,
Each in his narrow cell for ever laid,
The rude Forefathers of the hamlet sleep.

The breezy call of incense-breathing Morn,
The swallow twitt'ring from the straw-built shed,
The cock's shrill clarion, or the ecchoing horn,
No more shall rouse them from their lowly bed.

For them no more the blazing hearth shall burn,
Or busy housewife ply her evening care:
No children run to lisp their sire's return,
Or climb his knees the envied kiss to share.

Oft did the harvest to their sickle yield,
Their furrow oft the stubborn glebe has broke;
How jocund did they drive their team afield!
How bow'd the woods beneath their sturdy stroke!

Let not Ambition mock their useful toil,
Their homely joys, and destiny obscure;
Nor Grandeur hear with a disdainful smile,
The short and simple annals of the poor.

The boast of heraldry, the pomp of power,
And all that beauty, all that wealth e'er gave,
Await alike the inevitable hour.
The paths of glory lead but to the grave.

Thomas Gray (1716–1771)

Twilight (III)

A sumptuous splendour of leaves
Murmurously fanning the evening heaven;
And I hear
In the soft living grey shadows,
In the brooding evanescent atmosphere,
The voice of impatient night.

The splendour shall vanish in a vaster splendour;
Its own identity shall lose itself,
And the golden glory of day
Give birth to the glimmering face of the twilight,
And she shall grow into a vast enormous pearl maiden
Whose velvet tresses shall envelop the world –
Night.

Isaac Rosenberg (1890–1918)

To a Daisy

Slight as thou art, thou art enough to hide,
  Like all created things, secrets from me,
  And stand a barrier to eternity.
And I, how can I praise thee well and wide
From where I dwell – upon the hither side?
  Thou little veil for so great mystery,
  When shall I penetrate all things and thee,
And then look back? For this I must abide,

Till thou shalt grow and fold and be unfurled
Literally between me and the world.
  Then I shall drink from in beneath a spring,
And from a poet's side shall read his book.
O daisy mine, what will it be to look
  From God's side even of such a simple thing?

Alice Meynell (1847–1922)

The Sea-bird's Cry

'Tis harsh to hear, from ledge or peak,
The sunny cormorant's tuneless shriek;
Fierce songs they chant, in pool or cave,
Dark wanderers of the western wave.
Here will the listening landsman pray
For memory's music, far away;
Soft throats that nestling by the rose,
Soothe the glad rivulet as it flows.

Cease, stranger! cease that fruitless word,
Give eve's hushed bough to woodland bird:
Let the winged minstrel's valley-note
'Mid flowers and fragrance, pause and float.
Here must the echoing beak prevail,
To pierce the storm and cleave the gale;
To call, when warring tides shall foam,
The fledgeling of the waters home.

Wild things are here of sea and land,
Stern surges and a haughty strand;
Sea-monsters haunt yon caverned lair,
The mermaid wrings her briny hair.
That cry, those sullen accents sound
Like native echoes of the ground.
Lo! He did all things well Who gave
The sea-bird's voice to such a wave.

Rev. Robert Stephen Hawker, Vicar of Morwenstow (1803–1875)

Bonie Doon

Ye flowery banks o' bonie Doon,
  How can ye blume sae fair?
How can ye chant, ye little birds,
  And I sae fu' o' care?

Thou'll break my heart, thou bonie bird,
  That sings upon the bough;
Thou minds me o' the happy days,
  When my fause luve was true.

Thou'll break my heart, thou bonie bird,
  That sings beside thy mate;
For sae I sat, and sae I sang,
  And wist na o' my fate.

Aft hae I roved by bonie Doon
  To see the wood-bine twine,
And ilka bird sang o' its luve,
  And sae did I o' mine.

Wi' lightsome heart I pu'd a rose
  Frae aff its thorny tree;
And my fause luver staw my rose
  But left the thorn wi' me.

Robert Burns (1759–1796)

The Bat

The Bat is dun, with wrinkled Wings –
Like fallow Article –
And not a song pervade his Lips –
Or none perceptible.

His small Umbrella quaintly halved
Describing in the Air
An Arc alike inscrutable
Elate Philosopher.

Deputed from what Firmament –
Of what Astute Abode –
Empowered with what Malignity
Auspiciously withheld –

To his adroit Creator
Ascribe no less the praise –
Beneficent, believe me,
His Eccentricities –

Emily Dickinson (1830–1886)

An August Midnight

I

A shaded lamp and a waving blind,
And the beat of a clock from a distant floor:
On this scene enter – winged, horned, and spined –
A longlegs, a moth, and a dumbledore;
While 'mid my page there idly stands
A sleepy fly, that rubs its hands ...

II

Thus meet we five, in this still place,
At this point of time, at this point in space.
– My guests besmear my new-penned line,
Or bang at the lamp and fall supine.
'God's humblest, they!' I muse. Yet why?
They know Earth-secrets that know not I.

Thomas Hardy (1840–1928)

The Butterfly Trainers

Butterflies didn't always know
How to spread their wings and go
Gliding down the slopes of air
On their spangled wings and fair;
Never dared to leave the land
Till the elves took them in hand,
Made them bridle, bit and reins
Out of shiny corn silk skeins;
Drove them through the long blue hours,
Introducing them to Flowers.

Rachel Field (1894–1942)

Sonnet

The silver mist more lowly swims
And each green bosomed valley dims
And o'er the neighbouring meadow lies
Like half seen visions by dim eyes
Green trees look grey, bright waters black
The lated crow has lost her track
And flies by guess her journey home

She flops along and cannot see
Her peaceful nest on odlin tree
The lark drops down and cannot meet
The taller black grown clumps of wheat
The mists that rise from heat of day
Fades fields and meadows all away

John Clare (1793–1864)

The Dor-Hawk

VERSES 1–5

Fern-owl, Churn-owl, or Goat-sucker,
Night-jar, Dor-hawk, or whate'er
Be thy name among a dozen, –
Whip-poor-Will's and Who-are-you's cousin,
Chuck-Will's-widow's near relation,
Thou art at thy night vocation,
Thrilling the still evening air!

In the dark brown wood beyond us,
Where the night lies dusk and deep;
Where the fox his burrow maketh,
Where the tawny owl awaketh
Nightly from his day-long sleep;

There Dor-hawk is thy abiding,
Meadow green is not for thee;
While the aspen branches shiver,
'Mid the roaring of the river,
Comes thy chirring voice to me.

Bird, thy form I never looked on,
And to see it do not care;
Thou hast been, and thou art only
As a voice of forests lonely,
Heard and dwelling only there.

Bringing thoughts of dusk and shadow;
 Trees huge-branched in ceaseless change;
Pallid night-moths, spectre-seeming;
All a silent land of dreaming,
 Indistinct and large and strange.

Mary Howitt (1799–1888)

I know a Bank Where the Wild Thyme Blows

FROM *A MIDSUMMER NIGHT'S DREAM,* ACT II, SCENE I

I know a bank where the wild thyme blows,
Where oxlips and the nodding violet grows,
Quite overcanopied with luscious woodbine,
With sweet musk-roses, and with eglantine:
There sleeps Titania sometime of the night,
Lulled in these flowers with dances and delight.

William Shakespeare (1564–1616)

To a Squirrel at Kyle-na-no

Come play with me;
Why should you run
Through the shaking tree
As though I'd a gun
To strike you dead?
When all I would do
Is to scratch your head
And let you go.

W. B. Yeats (1865–1939)

Meeting at Night

I

The grey sea and the long black land;
And the yellow half-moon large and low;
And the startled little waves that leap
In fiery ringlets from their sleep,
As I gain the cove with pushing prow,
And quench its speed in the slushy sand.

II

Then a mile of warm sea-scented beach;
Three fields to cross till a farm appears;
A tap at the pane, the quick sharp scratch
And blue spurt of a lighted match,
And a voice less loud, thro' its joys and fears,
Than the two hearts beating each to each!

Robert Browning (1812–1889)

26 AUGUST

Between the Dusk of a Summer Night

PRAELUDIUM, XXII

Between the dusk of a summer night
  And the dawn of a summer day,
We caught at a mood as it passed in flight,
  And we bade it stoop and stay.
And what with the dawn of night began
  With the dusk of day was done;
For that is the way of woman and man,
  When a hazard has made them one.

Arc upon arc, from shade to shine,
  The World went thundering free;
And what was his errand but hers and mine –
  The lords of him, I and she?
O, it's die we must, but it's live we can,
  And the marvel of earth and sun
Is all for the joy of woman and man
  And the longing that makes them one.

W. E. Henley (1849–1903)

On a Wet Summer

All ye who, far from town, in rural hall,
  Like me were wont to dwell near pleasant field,
  Enjoying all the sunny day did yield,
  With me the change lament, in irksome thrall,
By rains incessant held; for now no call
  From early swain invites my hand to wield
  The scythe; in parlour dim I sit concealed,
  And mark the lessening sand from hourglass fall,
Or 'neath my window view the wistful train
  Of dripping poultry, whom the vine's broad leaves
  Shelter no more. – Mute is the mournful plain,
Silent the swallow sits beneath the thatch,
  And vacant hind hangs pensive o'er his hatch,
  Counting the frequent drips from reeded eaves.

James Bampfylde (1754–1796)

The Yellow-hammer

When, towards the summer's close,
  Lanes are dry,
And unclipt the hedgethorn rows,
  There we fly!

While the harvest waggons pass
  With their load,
Shedding corn upon the grass
  By the road,

In a flock we follow them,
  On and on,
Seize a wheat-ear by the stem,
  And are gone …

With our funny little song,
  Thus you may
Often see us flit along,
  Day by day.

Thomas Hardy (1840–1928)

29 AUGUST

Sea Calm

How still,
How strangely still
The water is today.
It is not good
For water
To be so still that way.

·

Langston Hughes (1901–1967)

The Things that Grow

It was nothing but a little neglected garden,
Laurel-screened, and hushed in a hot stillness;
An old pear-tree, and flowers mingled with weeds.
Yet as I came to it all unawares, it seemed
Charged with mystery; and I stopped, intruding,
Fearful of hurting that so absorbed stillness.
For I was tingling with the wind's salty splendour,
And still my senses moved with the keel's buoyance
Out on the water, where strong light was shivered
Into a dance dazzling as drops of flame.
The rocking radiance and the winged sail's lifting
And the noise of the rush of the water left behind
Sang to my body of movement, victory, joy.
But here the light was asleep, and green, green
In a veined leaf it glowed among the shadows.
A hollyhock rose to the sun and bathed its flowers
Luminously clustered in the unmoving air;
A butterfly lazily winked its gorgeous wings;
Marigolds burned intently amid the grass;
The ripening pears hung each with a rounded shadow:
All beyond was drowned in the indolent blueness;
And at my feet, like a word of an unknown tongue,
Was the midnight-dark bloom of the delicate pansy.
Suddenly these things awed my heart, as if here
In perishing blossom and springing shoot were a power
Greater than shipwrecking winds and all wild waters.

Laurence Binyon (1869–1943)

Who Has Seen the Wind?

Who has seen the wind?
  Neither I nor you:
But when the leaves hang trembling,
  The wind is passing thro'.

Who has seen the wind?
  Neither you nor I:
But when the trees bow down their heads,
  The wind is passing by.

Christina Rossetti (1830–1894)

SEPTEMBER

Colder Airs Creeping from the Misty Moon

1 SEPTEMBER

Autumn

FROM *THE LAND*

Now I have told the year from dawn to dusk,
Its morning and its evening and its noon;
Once round the sun our slanting orbit rolled,
Four times the seasons changed, thirteen the moon;
Corn grew from seed to husk,
The young spring grass for provender for herds;
Drought came, and earth was grateful for the rain;
The bees streamed in and out the summer hives;
Birds wildly sang; were silent; birds
With summer's passing fitfully sang again;
The loaded waggon crossed the field; the sea
Spread her great generous pasture as a robe
Whereon the slow ships, circling statelily,
Are patterned round the globe.
The ample busyness of life went by,
All the full busyness of lives
Unknown to fame, made lovely by no words:
The shepherd lonely in the winter fold;
The tiller following the eternal plough
Beneath a stormy or a gentle sky;
The sower with his gesture like a gift
Walking the furrowed hill from base to brow;
The reaper in the piety of thrift
Binding the sheaf against his slanted thigh.

Vita Sackville-West (1892–1962)

Autumn Song

Autumn clouds are flying, flying
  O'er the waste of blue;
Summer flowers are dying, dying,
  Late so lovely new.
Labouring wains are slowly rolling
  Home with winter grain;
Holy bells are slowly tolling
  Over buried men.

Goldener light sets noon a sleeping
  Like an afternoon;
Colder airs come stealing, creeping
  From the misty moon;
And the leaves, of old age dying,
  Earthy hues put on;
Out on every lone wind sighing
  That their day is gone.

Autumn's sun is sinking, sinking
  Down to winter low;
And our hearts are thinking, thinking
  Of the sleet and snow;
For our sun is slowly sliding
  Down the hill of might;
And no moon is softly gliding
  Up the slope of night.

See the bare fields' pillaged prizes
  Heaped in golden glooms!
See, the earth's outworn sunrises
  Dream in cloudy tombs!
Darkling flowers but wait the blowing
  Of a quickening wind;
And the man, through Death's door going,
  Leaves old Death behind.

Mourn not, then, clear tones that alter;
  Let the gold turn gray;
Feet, though feeble, still may falter
  Toward the better day!
Brother, let not weak faith linger
  O'er a withered thing;
Mark how Autumn's prophet finger
  Burns to hues of Spring.

George MacDonald (1824–1905)

Autumn

Autumn comes laden with her ripened load
Of fruitage and so scatters them abroad
That each fern smothered heath and molehill waste
Are black with bramble berrys – where in haste
The chubby urchins from the village hie
To feast them there stained with the purple dye
While painted woods around my rambles be
In draperies worthy of eternity
Yet will the leaves soon patter on the ground
And deaths deaf voice awake at every sound
One drops – then others – and the last that fell
Rings for those left behind their passing bell
Thus memory every where her tidings brings
How sad death robs us of lifes dearest things

John Clare (1793–1864)

To Autumn

I

Season of mists and mellow fruitfulness,
  Close bosom-friend of the maturing sun;
Conspiring with him how to load and bless
  With fruit the vines that round the thatch-eves run;
To bend with apples the moss'd cottage-trees,
  And fill all fruit with ripeness to the core;
    To swell the gourd, and plump, the hazel shells
  With a sweet kernel; to set budding more,
And still more, later flowers for the bees,
Until they think warm days will never cease,
  For Summer has o'er-brimmed their clammy cells.

II

Who hath not seen thee oft amid thy store?
  Sometimes whoever seeks abroad may find
Thee sitting careless on a granary floor,
  Thy hair soft-lifted by the winnowing wind;
Or on a half-reap'd furrow sound asleep,
  Drows'd with the fume of poppies, while thy hook
    Spares the next swathe and all its twined flowers:
And sometimes like a gleaner thou dost keep
  Steady thy laden head across a brook;
  Or by a cyder-press, with patient look,
    Thou watchest the last oozing hours by hours.

III

Where are the songs of Spring? Ay, where are they?
  Think not of them, thou hast thy music too, –
While barred clouds bloom the soft-dying day,
  And touch the stubble-plains with rosy hue;
Then in a wilful choir the small gnats mourn
  Among the river sallows, borne aloft
    Or sinking as the light wind lives or dies;
And full-grown lambs loud bleat from hilly bourn;
  Hedge-crickets sing; and now with treble soft
  The red-breast whistles from a garden-croft;
    And gathering swallows twitter in the skies.

John Keats (1795–1821)

September Day

(PONT DE NEUILLY)

The Seine flows out of the mist
  And into the mist again;
The trees lean over the water,
  The small leaves fall like rain.

The leaves fall patiently,
  Nothing remembers or grieves;
The river takes to the sea
  The yellow drift of the leaves.

Milky and cold is the air,
  The leaves float with the stream,
The river comes out of a sleep
  And goes away in a dream.

Sara Teasdale (1884–1933)

Binsey Poplars

FELLED 1879

My aspens dear, whose airy cages quelled,
Quelled or quenched in leaves the leaping sun,
  Áll félled, félled, are áll félled;
  Of a fresh and following folded rank
                Not spared, not one
                That dandled a sandalled
        Shadow that swam or sank
On meadow and river and wind-wandering weed winding bank.

O if we but knew what we do
        When we delve or hew –
  Hack and rack the growing green!
        Since Country is so tender
    To tóuch, her béing só slénder,
    That, like this sleek and seeing ball
    But a prick will make no eye at all,
    Where we, even where we mean
                To mend her we end her,
        When we hew or delve:
After-comers cannot guess the beauty been.
  Ten or twelve, only ten or twelve
    Strokes of havoc unselve
        The sweet especial scene,
    Rural scene, a rural scene,
    Sweet especial rural scene.

Gerard Manley Hopkins (1844–1889)

When Soft September Brings Again

When soft September brings again
  To yonder gorse its golden glow,
And Snowdon sends its autumn rain
  To bid thy current livelier flow;
Amid that ashen foliage light
When scarlet beads are glistering bright,
While alder boughs unchanged are seen
In summer livery of green;
When clouds before the cooler breeze
Are flying, white and large; with these
Returning, so I may return,
And find thee changeless, Pont-y-wern.

Arthur Hugh Clough (1819–1861)

The Deserted Garden

VERSES 1–6

I mind me in the days departed,
How often underneath the sun
With childish bounds I used to run
  To a garden long deserted.

The beds and walks were vanished quite;
And wheresoe'er had struck the spade,
The greenest grasses Nature laid,
  To sanctify her right.

I called the place my wilderness,
For no one entered there but I;
The sheep looked in, the grass to espy,
  And passed it ne'ertheless.

The trees were interwoven wild,
And spread their boughs enough about
To keep both sheep and shepherd out,
  But not a happy child.

Adventurous joy it was for me!
I crept beneath the boughs, and found
A circle smooth of mossy ground
  Beneath a poplar tree.

Old garden rose-trees hedged it in,
Bedropt with roses waxen-white,
Well satisfied with dew and light,
   And careless to be seen.

Elizabeth Barrett Browning (1806–1861)

Ode to the West Wind

PART I

O wild West Wind, thou breath of Autumn's being,
Thou, from whose unseen presence the leaves dead
Are driven, like ghosts from an enchanter fleeing,

Yellow, and black, and pale, and hectic red,
Pestilence-stricken multitudes: O thou,
Who chariotest to their dark wintry bed

The wingèd seeds, where they lie cold and low,
Each like a corpse within its grave, until
Thine azure sister of the Spring shall blow

Her clarion o'er the dreaming earth, and fill
(Driving sweet buds like flocks to feed in air)
With living hues and odours plain and hill:

Wild Spirit, which art moving everywhere;
Destroyer and preserver; hear, oh, hear!

Percy Bysshe Shelley (1792–1822)

Autumn

All day I have watched the purple vine leaves
Fall into the water.
And now in the moonlight they still fall,
But each leaf is fringed with silver.

Amy Lowell (1874–1925)

Twilight Time

LINES 1–24

And now the trembling light
Glimmers behind the little hills and corn,
Lingering as loath to part. Yet part thou must,
And though than open day far pleasing more
(Ere yet the fields and pearlèd cups of flowers
        Twinkle in the parting light),
Thee night shall hide, sweet visionary gleam
That softly lookest through the rising dew –
        Till, all like silver bright.
      The Faithful Witness, pure and white
      Shall look o'er yonder grassy hill,
        At this village, safe and still.
        All is safe and all is still,
      Save what noise the watch-dog makes
        Or the shrill cock the silence breaks
        Now and then –
        And now and then –
        Hark! once again,
        The wether's bell to us doth tell
        Some little stirring in the fold.
        Methinks the lingering, dying ray
            Of twilight time doth seem more fair.
      And lights the soul up more than day,
        When wide-spread, sultry sunshines are . . .

Samuel Palmer (1805–1863)

Remembrance of Nature

Oh Nature thou didst rear me for thine own,
With thy free singing-birds and mountain-brooks,
Feeding my thoughts in primrose-haunted nooks
With fairy fantasies and wood-dreams lone;
And thou didst teach me every wandering tone
Drawn from thy many-whispering trees and waves,
And guide my steps to founts and sparry caves,
And where bright mosses wove thee a rich throne
Midst the green hills. And now that, far estranged
From all sweet sounds and odours of thy breath,
Fading I lie, within my heart unchanged
So glows the love of thee that not for death
Seems that pure passion's fervour, but ordained
To meet on brighter shores thy majesty unstained.

Felicia Hemans (1793–1835)

Something Told the Wild Geese

Something told the wild geese
  It was time to go.
Though the fields lay golden
  Something whispered, – 'Snow.'
Leaves were green and stirring,
  Berries, luster-glossed,
But beneath warm feathers
  Something cautioned, – 'Frost.'
All the sagging orchards
  Steamed with amber spice,
But each wild breast stiffened
  At remembered ice.
Something told the wild geese
  It was time to fly, –
Summer sun was on their wings,
  Winter in their cry.

Rachel Field (1894–1942)

September

The dark green Summer, with its massive hues.
Fades into Autumn's tincture manifold.
A gorgeous garniture of fire and gold
The high slope of the ferny hill indues.
The mists of morn in slumbering layers diffuse
O'er glimmering rock, smooth lake, and spiked array
Of hedge-row thorns, a unity of grey.
All things appear their tangible form to lose
In ghostly vastness. But anon the gloom
Melts, as the Sun puts off his muddy veil;
And now the birds their twittering songs resume.
All Summer silent in the leafy dale.
In Spring they piped of love on every tree.
But now they sing the song of memory.

Hartley Coleridge (1796–1849)

The Road Not Taken

Two roads diverged in a yellow wood,
And sorry I could not travel both
And be one traveller, long I stood
And looked down one as far as I could
To where it bent in the undergrowth;

Then took the other, as just as fair,
And having perhaps the better claim,
Because it was grassy and wanted wear;
Though as for that the passing there
Had worn them really about the same,

And both that morning equally lay
In leaves no step had trodden black.
Oh, I kept the first for another day!
Yet knowing how way leads on to way,
I doubted if I should ever come back.

I shall be telling this with a sigh
Somewhere ages and ages hence:
Two roads diverged in a wood, and I –
I took the one less travelled by,
And that has made all the difference.

Robert Frost (1874–1963)

Sudden Shower

Black grows the southern clouds betokening rain
And humming hive bees homeward hurry bye
They feel the change – so let us shun the grain
And take the broad road while our feet are dry
Aye there some dropples moistened in my face
And pattered on my hat – tis coming nigh
Lets look about and find a sheltering place
The little things around like you and I
Are hurrying thro the grass to shun the shower
Here stoops an Ash tree – hark the wind gets high
But never mind its Ivy for an hour
Rain as it may will keep us dryly here
That little Wren knows well his sheltering bower
Nor leaves his dry house tho we come so near

John Clare (1793–1864)

17 SEPTEMBER

Songs of the Autumn Nights

SONG I

O night, send up the harvest moon
  To walk about the fields,
And make of midnight magic noon
  On lonely tarns and wealds.

In golden ranks, with golden crowns,
  All in the yellow land,
Old solemn kings in rustling gowns,
  The shocks moon-charmed stand.

Sky-mirror she, afloat in space,
  Beholds our coming morn:
Her heavenly joy hath such a grace,
  It ripens earthly corn;

Like some lone saint with upward eyes,
  Lost in the deeps of prayer:
The people still their prayers and sighs,
  And gazing ripen there.

George MacDonald (1824–1905)

The Autumn Crocus

In the high woods that crest our hills,
Upon a steep, rough slope of forest ground,
Where few flowers grow, sweet blooms today I found
Of the Autumn Crocus, blowing pale and fair.
Dim falls the sunlight there;
And a mild fragrance the lone thicket fills.

Languidly curved, the long white stems
Their purple flowers' gold treasure scarce display:
Lost were their leaves since in the distant spring,
Their February sisters showed so gay.
Roses of June, ye too have followed fleet!
Forsaken now, and shaded as by thought,
As by the human shade of thought and dreams,
They bloom 'mid the dark wood, whose air has wrought
With what soft nights and mornings of still dew!
Into their slender petals that clear hue,
Like paleness in fresh cheeks; a thing
On earth, I vowed, ne'er grew
More delicately pure, more shyly sweet.
Child of the pensive autumn woods!
So lovely, though thou dwell obscure and lone,
And though thy flush and gaiety be gone;
Say, among flowers of the sad, human mind,
Where shall I ever find
So rare a grace? in what shy solitudes?

Laurence Binyon (1869–1943)

On Esthwaite Water

VERSES 1–5

O'er Esthwaite's lake, serene and still,
  At sunset's silent peaceful hour
Scarce moved the zephyr's softest breath,
  Or sighed along its reedy shore.

The lovely landscape on its sides,
  With evening's softening hues impressed,
Shared in the general calm, and gave
  Sweet visions of repose and rest.

Inverted on the waveless flood,
  A spotless mirror smooth and clear,
Each fair surrounding object shone
  In softer beauty imaged there.

Brown hills and woods of various shades,
  Orchards and sloping meadows green,
Sweet rural seats and sheltered farms,
  Were in the bright reflector seen.

E'en lofty Tilberthwaite from far
  His giant shadow boldly threw,
His ruggéd, dark, high-towering head
  On Esthwaite's tranquil breast to view.

Isabella Lickbarrow (1784–1847)

Apple-Trees

When autumn stains and dapples
The diverse land,
Thickly studded with apples
The apple-trees stand.

Their mystery none discovers,
So none can tell –
Not the most passionate lovers
Of garth and fell;
For the silent sunlight weaves
The orchard spell,
Bough, bole, and root,
Mysterious, hung with leaves,
Embossed with fruit.

Though merle and throstle were loud,
Silent *their* passion in spring,
A blush of blossom wild-scented;
And now when no song-birds sing.
They are heavy with apples and proud
And supremely contented –
All fertile and green and sappy,
No wish denied,
Exceedingly quiet and happy
And satisfied!

No jealousy, anger, or fashion
Of strife
Perturbs in their stations
The apple-trees. Life
Is an effortless passion,
Fruit, bough, and stem,
A beautiful patience
For them.

Frost of the harvest-moon
Changes their sap to wine;
Ruddy and golden soon
Their clustered orbs will shine,
By favour
Of many a wind,
Of morn and noon and night,
Fulfilled from core to rind
With savour
Of all delight.

John Davidson (1857–1909)

Pied Beauty

Glory be to God for dappled things –
For skies of couple-colour as a brinded cow;
For rose-moles all in stipple upon trout that swim;
Fresh-firecoal chestnut-falls; finches' wings;
Landscape plotted and pieced – fold, fallow, and plough;
And áll trades, their gear and tackle and trim.

All things counter, original, spáre, strange;
Whatever is fickle, frecklèd (who knows how?)
With swíft, slów; sweet, sóur; adázzle, dím;
He fathers-forth whose beauty is pást change:
Práise him.

Gerard Manley Hopkins (1844–1889)

The Harvest Moon

The flame-red moon, the harvest moon,
Rolls along the hills, gently bouncing,
A vast balloon,
Till it takes off, and sinks upward
To lie in the bottom of the sky, like a gold doubloon.

The harvest moon has come,
Booming softly through heaven, like a bassoon.
And earth replies all night, like a deep drum.

So people can't sleep,
So they go out where elms and oak trees keep
A kneeling vigil, in a religious hush.
The harvest moon has come!

And all the moonlit cows and all the sheep
Stare up at her petrified, while she swells
Filling heaven, as if red hot, and sailing
Closer and closer like the end of the world.

Till the gold fields of stiff wheat
Cry 'We are ripe, reap us!' and the rivers
Sweat from the melting hills.

Ted Hughes (1930–1998)

Diary of a Church Mouse

Here among long-discarded cassocks,
Damp stools, and half-split open hassocks,
Here where the Vicar never looks
I nibble through old service books.
Lean and alone I spend my days
Behind this Church of England baize.
I share my dark forgotten room
With two oil-lamps and half a broom.
The cleaner never bothers me,
So here I eat my frugal tea.
My bread is sawdust mixed with straw;
My jam is polish for the floor.
Christmas and Easter may be feasts
For congregations and for priests,
And so may Whitsun. All the same,
They do not fill my meagre frame.
For me the only feast at all
Is Autumn's Harvest Festival,
When I can satisfy my want
With ears of corn around the font.
I climb the eagle's brazen head
To burrow through a loaf of bread.
I scramble up the pulpit stair
And gnaw the marrows hanging there.
It is enjoyable to taste
These items ere they go to waste,

But how annoying when one finds
That other mice with pagan minds
Come into church my food to share
Who have no proper business there.
Two field mice who have no desire
To be baptized, invade the choir.
A large and most unfriendly rat
Comes in to see what we are at.
He says he thinks there is no God
And yet he comes ... it's rather odd.
This year he stole a sheaf of wheat
(It screened our special preacher's seat),
And prosperous mice from fields away
Come in to hear our organ play,
And under cover of its notes
Ate through the altar's sheaf of oats.
A Low Church mouse, who thinks that I
Am too papistical, and High,
Yet somehow doesn't think it wrong
To munch through Harvest Evensong,
While I, who starve the whole year through,
Must share my food with rodents who
Except at this time of the year
Not once inside the church appear.
Within the human world I know
Such goings-on could not be so,

For human beings only do
What their religion tells them to.
They read the Bible every day
And always, night and morning, pray,
And just like me, the good church mouse,
Worship each week in God's own house,
But all the same it's strange to me
How very full the church can be
With people I don't see at all
Except at Harvest Festival.

John Betjeman (1906–1984)

The Owl

When cats run home and light is come,
  And dew is cold upon the ground,
And the far-off stream is dumb,
  And the whirring sail goes round,
  And the whirring sail goes round;
    Alone and warming his five wits,
    The white owl in the belfry sits.

When merry milkmaids click the latch,
  And rarely smells the new-mown hay,
And the cock hath sung beneath the thatch
  Twice or thrice his roundelay,
  Twice or thrice his roundelay;
    Alone and warming his five wits,
    The white owl in the belfry sits.

Alfred, Lord Tennyson (1809–1892)

The Solitary Reaper

Behold her, single in the field,
Yon solitary Highland Lass!
Reaping and singing by herself;
Stop here, or gently pass!
Alone she cuts and binds the grain,
And sings a melancholy strain;
O listen! for the Vale profound
Is overflowing with the sound.

No Nightingale did ever chaunt
So sweetly to reposing bands
Of Travellers in some shady haunt,
Among Arabian Sands:
No sweeter voice was ever heard
In spring-time from the Cuckoo-bird,
Breaking the silence of the seas
Among the farthest Hebrides.

Will no one tell me what she sings? –
Perhaps the plaintive numbers flow
For old, unhappy, far-off things,
And battles long ago:
Or is it some more humble lay,
Familiar matter of to-day?
Some natural sorrow, loss, or pain,
That has been, and may be again?

Whate'er the theme, the Maiden sang
As if her song could have no ending;
I saw her singing at her work,
And o'er the sickle bending;
I listened till I had my fill:
And, as I mounted up the hill,
The music in my heart I bore,
Long after it was heard no more.

William Wordsworth (1770–1850)

Late September

Tang of fruitage in the air;
Red boughs bursting everywhere;
Shimmering of seeded grass;
Hooded gentians all a'mass.

Warmth of earth, and cloudless wind
Tearing off the husky rind,
Blowing feathered seeds to fall
By the sun-baked, sheltering wall.

Beech trees in a golden haze;
Hardy sumachs all ablaze,
Glowing through the silver birches.
How that pine tree shouts and lurches!

From the sunny door-jamb high,
Swings the shell of a butterfly.
Scrape of insect violins
Through the stubble shrilly dins.

Every blade's a minaret
Where a small muezzin's set,
Loudly calling us to pray
At the miracle of day.

Then the purple-lidded night
Westering comes, her footsteps light
Guided by the radiant boon
Of a sickle-shaped new moon.

Amy Lowell (1874–1925)

27 SEPTEMBER

Tell Me Not Here, It Needs Not Saying

LAST POEMS XL

Tell me not here, it needs not saying,
  What tune the enchantress plays
In aftermaths of soft September
  Or under blanching mays,
For she and I were long acquainted
  And I knew all her ways.

On russet floors, by waters idle,
  The pine lets fall its cone;
The cuckoo shouts all day at nothing
  In leafy dells alone;
And traveller's joy beguiles in autumn
  Hearts that have lost their own.

On acres of the seeded grasses
  The changing burnish heaves;
Or marshalled under moons of harvest
  Stand still all night the sheaves;
Or beeches strip in storms for winter
  And stain the wind with leaves.

Possess, as I possessed a season,
  The countries I resign,
Where over elmy plains the highway
  Would mount the hills and shine,
And full of shade the pillared forest
  Would murmur and be mine.

For nature, heartless, witless nature,
  Will neither care nor know
What stranger's feet may find the meadow
  And trespass there and go,
Nor ask amid the dews of morning
  If they are mine or no.

A. E. Housman (1859–1936)

In the Woods

I was in the woods to-day,
  And the leaves were spinning there,
Rich apparelled in decay, –
  In decay more wholly fair
  Than in life they ever were.

Gold and rich barbaric red
  Freakt with pale and sapless vein,
Spinning, spinning, spun and sped
  With a little sob of pain
  Back to harbouring earth again.

Long in homely green they shone
  Through the summer rains and sun,
Now their humbleness is gone,
  Now their little season run,
  Pomp and pageantry begun.

Sweet was life, and buoyant breath,
  Lovely too; but for a day
Issues from the house of death
  Yet more beautiful array:
  Hark, a whisper – 'Come away.'

One by one they spin and fall,
  But they fall in regal pride:
Dying, do they hear a call
  Rising from an ebbless tide,
  And, hearing, are beatified?

John Drinkwater (1882–1937)

Bavarian Gentians

Not every man has gentians in his house
in Soft September, at slow, Sad Michaelmas.

Bavarian gentians, big and dark, only dark
darkening the daytime torch-like with the smoking
  blueness of Pluto's gloom,
ribbed and torch-like, with their blaze of darkness spread blue
down flattening into points, flattened under the sweep of
  white day
torch-flower of the blue-smoking darkness, Pluto's
  dark-blue daze,
black lamps from the halls of Dis, burning dark blue,
giving off darkness, blue darkness, as Demeter's pale lamps
  give off light,
lead me then, lead me the way.

Reach me a gentian, give me a torch!
let me guide myself with the blue, forked torch of a flower
down the darker and darker stairs, where blue is darkened
  on blueness,
even where Persephone goes, just now, from the frosted
  September
to the sightless realm where darkness is awake upon the dark
and Persephone herself is but a voice
or a darkness invisible enfolded in the deeper dark
of the arms Plutonic, and pierced with the passion of dense
  gloom,
among the splendour of torches of darkness, shedding
  darkness on the lost bride and her groom.

D. H. Lawrence (1885–1930)

Autumn Twilight: Grey and Gold

FROM *INTERMEZZO: PASTORAL*

The long September evening dies
In mist along the fields and lanes;
Only a few faint stars surprise
The lingering twilight as it wanes.

Night creeps across the darkening vale;
On the horizon tree by tree
Fades into shadowy skies as pale
As moonlight on a shadowy sea.

And, down the mist-enfolded lanes,
Grown pensive now with evening,
See, lingering as the twilight wanes,
Lover with lover wandering.

Arthur Symons (1865–1945)

OCTOBER

The Western Sun Withdraws

There is a Solemn Wind To-Night

There is a solemn wind to-night
  That sings of solemn rain;
The trees that have been quiet so long
  Flutter and start again.

The slender trees, the heavy trees,
  The fruit trees laden and proud,
Lift up their branches to the wind
  That cries to them so loud.

The little bushes and the plants
  Bow to the solemn sound,
And every tiniest blade of grass
Shakes on the quiet ground.

Katherine Mansfield (1888–1923)

Autumn

I saw old Autumn in the misty morn
Stand shadowless like Silence, listening
To silence, for no lonely bird would sing
Into his hollow ear from woods forlorn,
Nor lowly hedge nor solitary thorn; –
Shaking his languid locks all dewy bright
With tangled gossamer that fell by night,
  Pearling his coronet of golden corn.

Where are the songs of Summer? – With the sun,
Oping the dusky eyelids of the south,
Till shade and silence waken up as one,
And Morning sings with a warm odorous mouth.
Where are the merry birds? – Away, away,
On panting wings through the inclement skies,
  Lest owls should prey
  Undazzled at noonday,
And tear with horny beak their lustrous eyes.

Where are the blooms of Summer? – In the west,
Blushing their last to the last sunny hours,
When the mild Eve by sudden Night is prest
Like tearful Proserpine, snatch'd from her flow'rs
  To a most gloomy breast.
Where is the pride of Summer, – the green pine, –
The many, many leaves all twinkling? – Three
  On the moss'd elm; three on the naked lime

Trembling, – and one upon the old oak-tree!
  Where is the Dryad's immortality? –
Gone into mournful cypress and dark yew,
Or wearing the long gloomy Winter through
  In the smooth holly's green eternity.
The squirrel gloats on his accomplish'd hoard,
The ants have brimm'd their garners with ripe grain,
  And honey bees have stor'd
The sweets of Summer in their luscious cells;
The swallows all have wing'd across the main;
But here the Autumn melancholy dwells,
  And sighs her tearful spells
Amongst the sunless shadows of the plain.
  Alone, alone,
  Upon a mossy stone,
She sits and reckons up the dead and gone
With the last leaves for a love-rosary,
Whilst all the wither'd world looks drearily,
Like a dim picture of the drowned past
In the hush'd mind's mysterious far away,
Doubtful what ghostly thing will steal the last
Into that distance, grey upon the grey.
O go and sit with her, and be o'ershaded
Under the languid downfall of her hair:
She wears a coronal of flowers faded
Upon her forehead, and a face of care; –
There is enough of wither'd every where
To make her bower, – and enough of gloom;

There is enough of sadness to invite,
If only for the rose that died, whose doom
Is Beauty's, – she that with the living bloom
Of conscious cheeks most beautifies the light; –
There is enough of sorrowing, and quite
Enough of bitter fruits the earth doth bear, –
Enough of chilly droppings for her bowl;
Enough of fear and shadowy despair,
To frame her cloudy prison for the soul!

Thomas Hood (1799–1845)

Under the Woods

When these old woods were young
The thrushes' ancestors
As sweetly sung
In the old years.

There was no garden here,
Apples nor mistletoe;
No children dear
Ran to and fro.

New then was this thatched cot,
But the keeper was old,
And he had not
Much lead or gold.

Most silent beech and yew:
As he went round about
The woods to view
Seldom he shot.

But now that he is gone
Out of most memories;
Still lingers on
A stoat of his,

But one, shrivelled and green,
And with no scent at all,
And barely seen
On this shed wall.

Edward Thomas (1878–1917)

Autumn's Gold

Along the tops of all the yellow trees,
  The golden-yellow trees, the sunshine lies;
  And where the leaves are gone, long rays surprise
Lone depths of thicket with their brightnesses;
And through the woods, all waste of many a breeze,
  Cometh more joy of light for Poet's eyes –
  Green fields lying yellow underneath the skies,
And shining houses and blue distances.

By the roadside, like rocks of golden ore
  That make the western river-beds so bright,
  The briar and the furze are all alight!
Perhaps the year will be so fair no more,
  But now the fallen, falling leaves are gay,
  And autumn old has shone into a Day!

George MacDonald (1824–1905)

5 OCTOBER

Grongar Hill

LINES 57–83

Below me trees unnumbered rise,
Beautiful in various dyes:
The gloomy pine, the poplar blue,
The yellow beech, the sable yew,
The slender fir that taper grows,
The sturdy oak, with wide-spread boughs.
And beyond the purple grove,
Haunt of Phillis, queen of love!
Gaudy as the op'ning dawn,
Lies a long and level lawn,
On which a dark hill, steep and high,
Holds and charms the wand'ring eye!
Deep are his feet in Towy's flood,
His sides are cloathed with waving wood,
And ancient towers crown his brow,
That cast an awful look below;
Whose ragged walls the ivy creeps,
And with her arms from falling keeps;
So both a safety from the wind
In mutual dependence find.
'Tis now the raven's bleak abode;
'Tis now th' apartment of the toad;
And there the fox securely feeds;
And there the pois'nous adder breeds,
Concealed in ruins, moss, and weeds;
While, ever and anon, there falls
Huge heap of hoary mouldered walls.

John Dyer (1699–1758)

In Autumn

VERSES 1–5

The leaves are many under my feet,
  And drift one way.
Their scent of death is weary and sweet.
  A flight of them is in the grey
Where sky and forest meet.

The low winds moan for sad sweet years;
  The birds sing all for pain,
Of a common thing, to weary ears, –
  Only a summer's fate of rain,
And a woman's fate of tears.

I walk to love and life alone
  Over these mournful places,
Across the summer overthrown,
  The dead joys of these silent faces,
To claim my own.

I know his heart has beat to bright
  Sweet loves gone by;
I know the leaves that die to-night
  Once budded to the sky;
And I shall die from his delight.

O leaves, so quietly ending now,
  You heard the cuckoos sing.
And I will grow upon my bough
  If only for a Spring,
And fall when the rain is on my brow.

Alice Meynell (1847–1922)

October

The October water is like glass and scarcely flows.
Beside the red tree the swan spreads a long wing.
Rose hips too are reflected in the stream
Where the bird's sudden movement has made no sound.

Iris Murdoch (1919–1999)

Flower and Flame

Between the flowering and the flaming woods,
  All greening in the rain,
    The fields unfold;
  The sun upon the grain
    Outpours its gold,
And sweet with bloom and dew are nature's moods
Between the flowering and the flaming woods.

Between the flowering and the flaming woods
  The wind bemoans a host
    Of withered leaves;
  The winter is a ghost
    That grieves and grieves
Around a ruined house where none intrudes,
Between the flaming and the flowering woods.

O woods that break in flower or in flame,
  My wingèd days and hours
    Shall meet their doom
  Like to your leaves and flowers;
    Let not your bloom
And brightness put my flying years to shame.
O woods that break in flower or in flame!

Ethelwyn Wetherald (1857–1940)

Astrophil and Stella

VERSE 31

With how sad steps, O moon, thou climb'st the skies;
 How silently, and with how wan a face.
 What, may it be that even in heav'nly place
That busy archer his sharp arrows tries?
Sure, if that long-with-love-acquainted eyes
 Can judge of love, thou feel'st a lover's case;
 I read it in thy looks; thy languish'd grace
To me, that feel the like, thy state descries.
 Then, even of fellowship, O moon, tell me,
Is constant love deemed there but want of wit?
Are beauties there as proud as here they be?
Do they above love to be loved, and yet
 Those lovers scorn whom that love doth possess?
 Do they call virtue there ungratefulness?

Sir Philip Sidney (1554–1586)

God's World

O world, I cannot hold thee close enough!
  Thy winds, thy wide grey skies!
  Thy mists, that roll and rise!
Thy woods, this autumn day, that ache and sag
And all but cry with colour! That gaunt crag
To crush! To lift the lean of that black bluff!
World, World, I cannot get thee close enough!

Long have I known a glory in it all,
    But never knew I this;
    Here such a passion is
As stretcheth me apart, – Lord, I do fear
Thou'st made the world too beautiful this year;
My soul is all but out of me, – let fall
No burning leaf; prithee, let no bird call.

Edna St Vincent Millay (1892–1950)

A Sunset

Upon the mountain's edge with light touch resting
There a brief while the globe of splendour sits
   And seems a creature of this earth; but soon
      More changeful than the Moon
To wane fantastic his great orb submits.
Or cone or mow of fire: till sinking slowly
Even to a star at length he lessens wholly.

Abrupt, as Spirits vanish, he is sunk!
A soul-like breeze possesses all the wood.
   The boughs, the sprays have stood
As motionless as stands the ancient trunk!
But every leaf through all the forest flutters,
And deep the cavern of the fountain mutters.

Samuel Taylor Coleridge (1772–1834)

Field of Autumn

Slow moves the acid breath of noon
over the copper-coated hill,
slow from the wild crab's bearded breast
the palsied apples fall.

Like coloured smoke the day hangs fire,
taking the village without sound;
the vulture-headed sun lies low
chained to the violet ground.

The horse upon the rocky height
rolls all the valley in his eye,
but dares not raise his foot or move
his shoulder from the fly.

The sheep, snail-backed against the wall,
lifts her blind face but does not know
the cry her blackened tongue gives forth
is the first bleat of snow.

Each bird and stone, each roof and well
feels the gold foot of autumn pass;
each spider binds with glittering snare
the splintered bones of grass.

Slow moves the hour that sucks our life,
slow drops the late wasp from the pear,
the rose tree's thread of scent draws thin –
and the snaps upon the air.

Laurie Lee (1914–1997)

13 OCTOBER

Beachy Head

LINES 75–99

For now the sun is verging to the sea,
And as he westward sinks, the floating clouds
Suspended, move upon the evening gale,
And gathering round his orb, as if to shade
The insufferable brightness, they resign
Their gauzy whiteness; and more warmed, assume
All hues of purple. There, transparent gold
Mingles with ruby tints, and sapphire gleams,
And colours, such as nature through her works
Shows only in the ethereal canopy.
Thither aspiring Fancy fondly soars,
Wandering sublime thro' visionary vales,
Where bright pavilions rise, and trophies, fanned
By airs celestial; and adorned with wreaths
Of flowers that bloom amid elysian bowers.
Now bright, and brighter still the colours glow,
Till half the lustrous orb within the flood
Seems to retire: the flood reflecting still
Its splendour, and in mimic glory dressed;
Till the last ray shot upward, fires the clouds
With blazing crimson; then in paler light,
Long lines of tenderer radiance, lingering yield
To partial darkness; and on the opposing side
The early moon distinctly rising, throws
Her pearly brilliance on the trembling tide.

Charlotte Smith (1749–1806)

The Secret Strength of Things

MONT BLANC: LINES WRITTEN IN THE VALE OF CHAMOUNI
VERSE I

The everlasting universe of things
Flows through the mind, and rolls its rapid waves,
Now dark, now glittering, now reflecting gloom,
Now lending splendour, where from secret springs
The source of human thought its tribute brings
Of waters – with a sound but half its own,
Such as a feeble brook will oft assume,
In the wild woods, among the mountains lone,
Where waterfalls around it leap for ever,
Where woods and winds contend, and a vast river
Over its rocks ceaselessly bursts and raves.

Percy Bysshe Shelley (1792–1822)

To the Evening Star

Thou fair-hair'd angel of the evening,
Now, whilst the sun rests on the mountains, light
Thy bright torch of love; thy radiant crown
Put on, and smile upon our evening bed!
Smile on our loves, and while thou drawest the
Blue curtains of the sky, scatter thy silver dew
On every flower that shuts its sweet eyes
In timely sleep. Let thy west wind sleep on
The lake; speak silence with thy glimmering eyes,
And wash the dusk with silver. Soon, full soon,
Dost thou withdraw; then the wolf rages wide,
And then the lion glares through the dun forest:
The fleeces of our flocks are cover'd with
Thy sacred dew: protect them with thine influence.

William Blake (1757–1827)

The Secret of the Sea

Ah! what pleasant visions haunt me
  As I gaze upon the sea!
All the old romantic legends,
  All my dreams, come back to me.

Sails of silk and ropes of sandal,
  Such as gleam in ancient lore;
And the singing of the sailors,
  And the answer from the shore!

Most of all, the Spanish ballad
  Haunts me oft, and tarries long,
Of the noble Count Arnaldos
  And the sailor's mystic song.

Like the long waves on a sea-beach,
  Where the sand as silver shines,
With a soft, monotonous cadence,
  Flow its unrhymed lyric lines; –

Telling how the Count Arnaldos,
  With his hawk upon his hand,
Saw a fair and stately galley,
  Steering onward to the land; –

How he heard the ancient helmsman
  Chant a song so wild and clear,
That the sailing sea-bird slowly
  Poised upon the mast to hear,

Till his soul was full of longing,
  And he cried, with impulse strong, –
'Helmsman! for the love of heaven,
  Teach me, too, that wondrous song!'

'Wouldst thou,' – so the helmsman answered,
  'Learn the secret of the sea?
Only those who brave its dangers
  Comprehend its mystery!'

In each sail that skims the horizon,
  In each landward-blowing breeze,
I behold that stately galley,
  Hear those mournful melodies;

Till my soul is full of longing
  For the secret of the sea,
And the heart of the great ocean
  Sends a thrilling pulse through me.

Henry Wadsworth Longfellow (1807–1882)

17 OCTOBER

The Night-Walk

LINES 1–20

Awakes for me and leaps from shroud
All radiantly the moon's own night
Of folded showers in streamer cloud;
Our shadows down the highway white
Or deep in woodland woven-boughed,
With yon and yon a stem alight.

I see marauder runagates
Across us shoot their dusky wink;
I hear the parliament of chats
In haws beside the river's brink;
And drops the vole off alder-banks,
To push his arrow through the stream.
These busy people had our thanks
For tickling sight and sound, but theme
They were not more than breath we drew
Delighted with our world's embrace:
The moss-root smell where beeches grew,
And watered grass in breezy space;
The silken heights, of ghostly bloom
Among their folds, by distance draped.

George Meredith (1828–1909)

To a Black Greyhound

Shining black in the shining light,
  Inky black in the golden sun,
Graceful as the swallow's flight,
  Light as swallow, wingèd one,
Swift as driven hurricane –
  Double-sinewed stretch and spring,
Muffled thud of flying feet,
  See the black dog galloping,
  Hear his wild foot-beat.

See him lie when the day is dead,
  Black curves curled on the boarded floor.
Sleepy eyes, my sleepy-head –
  Eyes that were aflame before.
Gentle now, they burn no more;
  Gentle now and softly warm,
With the fire that made them bright
  Hidden – as when after storm
  Softly falls the night.

God of speed, who makes the fire –
  God of Peace, who lulls the same –
God who gives the fierce desire,
  Lust for blood as fierce as flame –
God who stands in Pity's name –
  Many may ye be or less,
Ye who rule the earth and sun:
  Gods of strength and gentleness,
  Ye are ever one.

Julian Grenfell (1888–1915)

Silver

Slowly, silently, now the moon
Walks the night in her silver shoon;
This way, and that, she peers, and sees
Silver fruit upon silver trees;
One by one the casements catch
Her beams beneath the silvery thatch;
Couched in his kennel, like a log,
With paws of silver sleeps the dog;
From their shadowy cote the white breasts peep
Of doves in a silver-feathered sleep;
A harvest mouse goes scampering by,
With silver claws, and silver eye;
And moveless fish in the water gleam,
By silver reeds in a silver stream.

Walter de la Mare (1873–1956)

20 OCTOBER

After Rain

See how upon bare twigs they lie,
Raindrops, lately of the sky –
Balls of crystal, rounder far
Than any earthen berries are.
Phantom fruits begot of air
Fashioned for no human fare.

Rachel Field (1894–1942)

The View

FROM *PROLOGUE TO GENERAL HAMLEY, THE CHARGE OF THE HEAVY BRIGADE AT BALACLAVA*, LINES 1–8

Our birches yellowing and from each
  The light leaf falling fast,
While squirrels from our fiery beech
  Were bearing off the mast,
You came, and look'd and loved the view
  Long-known and loved by me,
Green Sussex fading into blue
  With one gray glimpse of sea.

Alfred, Lord Tennyson (1809–1892)

Upon the Shore

Who has not walked upon the shore,
And who does not the morning know,
The day the angry gale is o'er,
The hour the wind has ceased to blow?

The horses of the strong southwest
Are pastured round his tropic tent,
Careless how long the ocean's breast
Sob on and sigh for passion spent.

The frightened birds, that fled inland
To house in rock and tower and tree,
Are gathering on the peaceful strand,
To tempt again the sunny sea;

Whereon the timid ships steal out
And laugh to find their foe asleep,
That lately scattered them about,
And drave them to the fold like sheep.

The snow-white clouds he northward chased
Break into phalanx, line, and band:
All one way to the south they haste,
The south, their pleasant fatherland.

From distant hills their shadows creep,
Arrive in turn and mount the lea,
And flit across the downs, and leap
Sheer off the cliff upon the sea;

And sail and sail far out of sight.
But still I watch their fleecy trains,
That piling all the south with light,
Dapple in France the fertile plains.

Robert Bridges (1844–1930)

My Orcha'd in Linden Lea

'Ithin the woodlands, flow'ry gleäded,
  By the woak tree's mossy moot,
The sheenen grass-bleädes, timber-sheäded,
  Now do quiver under voot ;
An' birds do whissle over head,
An' water's bubblen in its bed,
An' there vor me the apple tree
Do leän down low in Linden Lea.

When leaves that leätely wer a-springen
  Now do feäde 'ithin the copse,
An' païnted birds do hush their zingen
  Up upon the timber's tops;
An' brown-leav'd fruit's a-turnen red,
In cloudless zunsheen, over head,
Wi' fruit vor me, the apple tree
Do leän down low in Linden Lea.

Let other vo'k meäke money vaster
  In the aïr o' dark-room'd towns,
I don't dread a peevish meäster;
  Though noo man do heed my frowns,
I be free to goo abrode,
Or teäke ageän my homeward road
To where, vor me, the apple tree
Do leän down low in Linden Lea.

William Barnes (1801–1886)

The Sea-Limits

Consider the sea's listless chime:
  Time's self it is, made audible, –
  The murmur of the earth's own shell.
Secret continuance sublime
  Is the sea's end: our sight may pass
  No furlong further. Since time was,
This sound hath told the lapse of time.

No quiet, which is death's, - it hath
  The mournfulness of ancient life,
  Enduring always at dull strife.
As the world's heart of rest and wrath,
  Its painful pulse is in the sands.
  Last utterly, the whole sky stands,
Grey and not known, along its path.

Listen alone beside the sea,
  Listen alone among the woods;
  Those voices of twin solitudes
Shall have one sound alike to thee:
  Hark where the murmurs of thronged men
  Surge and sink back and surge again, –
Still the one voice of wave and tree.

Gather a shell from the strown beach
  And listen at its lips: they sigh
  The same desire and mystery,
The echo of the whole sea's speech.
  And all mankind is thus at heart
  Not anything but what thou art:
And Earth, Sea, Man, are all in each.

D. G. Rossetti (1828–1882)

His Lady's Eyes

FROM *CAELICA*

You little stars that live in skies,
  And glory in Apollo's glory,
In whose aspects conjoined lies
  The Heaven's will and Nature's story,
Joy to be likened to those eyes,
  Which eyes make all eyes glad or sorry;
For when you force thoughts from above,
These overrule your force by love.

And thou, O Love, which in these eyes
  Hast married Reason with Affection,
And made them saints of Beauty's skies,
Where joys are shadows of perfection,
Lend me thy wings that I may rise
  Up, not by worth but thy election;
For I have vowed, in strangest fashion
To love and never seek compassion.

Fulke Greville, Lord Brooke (1554–1628)

The Birch Tree

Touched with beauty, I stand still and gaze
In the autumn twilight. Yellow leaves and brown
The grass enriching, gleam, or waver down
From lime and elm: far-glimmering through the haze
The quiet lamps in order twinkle; dumb
And fair the park lies; faint the city's hum.

And I regret not June's impassioned prime,
When her deep lilies banqueted the air,
And this now ruined, then so fragrant lime
Cooled with clear green the heavy noon's high glare;
Nor flushed carnations, breathing hot July;
Nor April's thrush in the blithest songs of the year,
With brown bloom on the elms and dazzling sky;
So strange a charm there lingers in this austere
Resigning month, yielding to what must be.
Yet most, O delicate birch, I envy thee,
Child among trees! with silvery slender limbs
And purple sprays of drooping hair. Night dims
The grass; the great elms darken; no birds sing.
At last I sigh for the warmth and the fragrance flown.
But thou in the leafless twilight shinest alone,
Awaiting in ignorant trust the certain spring.

Laurence Binyon (1869–1943)

27 OCTOBER

The Western Sun Withdraws

FROM *AUTUMN, THE SEASONS*

The western sun withdraws the shorten'd day;
And humid Evening, gliding o'er the sky,
In her chill progress, to the ground condensed
The vapours throws. Where creeping waters ooze,
Where marshes stagnate, and where rivers wind,
Cluster the rolling fogs, and swim along
The dusky-mantled lawn. Meanwhile the moon
Full-orb'd, and breaking through the scatter'd clouds,
Shows her broad visage in the crimson'd east.
Turn'd to the sun direct, her spotted disk,
Where mountains rise, umbrageous dales descend,
And caverns deep, as optic tube descries,
A smaller earth, gives us his blaze again,
Void of its flame, and sheds a softer day.
Now through the passing cloud she seems to stoop,
Now up the pure cerulean rides sublime.
Wide the pale deluge floats, and streaming mild
O'er the sky'd mountain to the shadowy vale,
While rocks and floods reflect the quivering gleam,
The whole air whitens with a boundless tide
Of silver radiance, trembling round the world.

James Thomson (1700–1748)

Magpies in Picardy

The magpies in Picardy
Are more than I can tell.
They flicker down the dusty roads
And cast a magic spell
On the men who march through Picardy,
Through Picardy to hell.

(The blackbird flies with panic,
The swallow goes like light,
The finches move like ladies,
The owl floats by at night;
But the great and flashing magpie
He flies as artists might.)

A magpie in Picardy
Told me secret things –
Of the music in white feathers,
And the sunlight that sings
And dances in deep shadows –
He told me with his wings.

(The hawk is cruel and rigid,
He watches from a height;
The rook is slow and sombre,
The robin loves to fight;
But the great and flashing magpie
He flies as lovers might.)

He told me that in Picardy,
An age ago or more,
While all his fathers were still eggs,
These dusty highways bore
Brown singing soldiers marching out
Through Picardy to war.

He said that still through chaos
Works on the ancient plan,
And two things have altered not
Since first the world began –
The beauty of the wild green earth
And the bravery of man.

(For the sparrow flies unthinking
And quarrels in his flight;
The heron trails his legs behind,
The lark goes out of sight;
But the great and flashing magpie
He flies as poets might.)

T. P. Cameron Wilson (1891–1918)

29 OCTOBER

Autumn Birds

The wild duck startles like a sudden thought
And heron slow as if it might be caught
The flopping crows on weary wings go bye
And grey beard jackdaws noising as they flye
The crowds of starnels wiz and hurry bye
And darken like a cloud the evening sky
The larks like thunder rise and suthy round
Then drop and nestle in the stubble ground
The wild swan hurries high and noises loud
With white neck peering to the evening cloud
The weary rooks to distant woods are gone
With length of tail the magpie winnows on
To neighbouring tree, and leaves the distant crow
While small birds nestle in the edge below

John Clare (1793–1864)

Moonlit Apples

At the top of the house the apples are laid in rows,
And the skylight lets the moonlight in, and those
Apples are deep-sea apples of green. There goes
  A cloud on the moon in the autumn night.

A mouse in the wainscot scratches, and scratches, and then
There is no sound at the top of the house of men
Or mice; and the cloud is blown, and the moon again
  Dapples the apples with deep-sea light.

They are lying in rows there, under the gloomy beams;
On the sagging floor; they gather the silver streams
Out of the moon, those moonlit apples of dreams,
  And quiet is the steep stair under.

In the corridors under there is nothing but sleep.
And stiller than ever on orchard boughs they keep
Tryst with the moon, and deep is the silence, deep
  On moon-washed apples of wonder.

John Drinkwater (1882–1937)

The Fairies

VERSES 1–3

Up the airy mountain,
  Down the rushy glen,
We darent go a-hunting
  For fear of little men;
Wee folk, good folk,
  Trooping all together;
Green jacket, red cap,
  And white owl's feather!

Down along the rocky shore
  Some make their home,
They live on crispy pancakes
  Of yellow tide-foam;
Some in the reeds
  Of the black mountain lake,
With frogs for their watch-dogs,
  All night awake.

High on the hill-top
  The old King sits;
He is now so old and gray
  He's nigh lost his wits.
With a bridge of white mist
  Columbkill he crosses,
On his stately journeys
  From Slieveleague to Rosses;
Or going up with music
  On cold starry nights
To sup with the Queen
  Of the gay Northern Lights.

William Allingham (1824–1889)

NOVEMBER

Withered Sward and Wintry Sky

Marmion

INTRODUCTION TO CANTO FIRST, LINES 1–36
TO WILLIAM STEWART ROSE, ESQ. ASHESTIEL, ETTRICK FOREST

November's sky is chill and drear,
November's leaf is red and sear:
Late, gazing down the steepy linn
That hems our little garden in,
Low in its dark and narrow glen
You scarce the rivulet might ken,
So thick the tangled greenwood grew,
So feeble trill'd the streamlet through:
Now, murmuring hoarse, and frequent seen
Through bush and briar, no longer green,
An angry brook, it sweeps the glade,
Brawls over rock and wild cascade,
And foaming brown, with doubled speed,
Hurries its waters to the Tweed.

No longer Autumn's glowing red
Upon our forest hills is shed;
No more, beneath the evening beam,
Fair Tweed reflects their purple gleam:
Away hath passed the heather-bell
That bloom'd so rich on Needpath Fell;
Sallow his brow, and russet bare
Are now the sister-heights of Yair.
The sheep, before the pinching heaven,
To shelter'd dale and down are driven,

Where yet some faded herbage pines,
And yet a watery sunbeam shines:
In meek despondency they eye
The wither'd sward and wintry sky,
And far beneath their summer hill,
Stray sadly by Glenkinnon's rill:
The shepherd shifts his mantle's fold,
And wraps him closer from the cold;
His dogs no merry circles wheel,
But, shivering, follow at his heel;
A cowering glance they often cast,
As deeper moans the gathering blast.

Sir Walter Scott (1771–1832)

The Storm is Over

LINES 1–21

The storm is over, the land hushes to rest:
The tyrannous wind, its strength fordone,
Is fallen back in the west
To couch with the sinking sun.
The last clouds fare
With fainting speed, and their thin streamers fly
In melting drifts of the sky.
Already the birds in the air
Appear again; the rooks return to their haunt,
And one by one,
Proclaiming aloud their care,
Renew their peaceful chant.

Torn and shattered trees their branches again reset,
They trim afresh the fair
Few green and golden leaves withheld from the storm,
And awhile will be handsome yet.
To-morrow's sun shall caress
Their remnant of loveliness:
In quiet days for a time
Sad Autumn lingering warm
Shall humour their faded prime.

Robert Bridges (1844–1930)

Echoes

The sea laments
The livelong day,
Fringing its wastes of sand;
Cries back the wind from the whispering shore –
No words I understand:
Yet echoes in my heart a voice,
As far, as near, as these –
The wind that weeps,
The solemn surge
Of strange and lonely seas.

Walter de la Mare (1873–1956)

The Last Robin

The spring was red with robins,
  The summer gay with their song;
What doest thou here at the bleak of the year,
  When the frost is sharp and strong,
When even the red from the leaves has fled,
  And the stormy night is long?

Silent, alone, thou givest
  An April gleam to the lane;
A sense of spring to the sorrowing
  Of autumn wind and rain.
Dear gleam, good-bye! the dark is nigh;
  Good-bye – come back again!

Ethelwyn Wetherald (1857–1940)

Beachy Head

LINES 368–389

Ah! hills so early loved! in fancy still
I breathe your pure keen air; and still behold
Those widely spreading views, mocking alike
The poet and the painter's utmost art.
And still, observing objects more minute,
Wondering remark the strange and foreign forms
Of seashells; with the pale calcareous soil
Mingled, and seeming of resembling substance.
Tho' surely the blue ocean 'from the heights
Where the Downs westward trend, but dimly seen'
Here never rolled its surge. Does nature then
Mimic, in wanton mood, fantastic shapes
Of bivalves, and inwreathed volutes, that cling
To the dark sea-rock of the wat'ry world?
Or did this range of chalky mountains, once
Form a vast basin, where the ocean waves
Swelled fathomless? What time these fossil shells,
Buoyed on their native element, were thrown
Among the imbedding calx: when the huge hill
Its giant bulk heaved, and in strange ferment
Grew up a guardian barrier, 'twixt the sea
And the green level of the sylvan weald.

Charlotte Smith (1749–1806)

November

FROM *THE EARTHLY PARADISE*

Are thine eyes weary? is thy heart too sick
To struggle any more with doubt and thought,
Whose formless veil draws darkening now and thick
Across thee, e'en as smoke-tinged mist-wreaths brought
Down a fair dale to make it blind and nought?
Art thou so weary that no world there seems
Beyond these four walls, hung with pain and dreams?

Look out upon the real world, where the moon,
Half-way 'twixt root and crown of these high trees,
Turns the dead midnight into dreamy noon,
Silent and full of wonders, for the breeze
Died at the sunset, and no images,
No hopes of day, are left in sky or earth –
Is it not fair, and of most wondrous worth?

Yea, I have looked, and seen November there;
The changeless seal of change it seemed to be,
Fair death of things that, living once, were fair;
Bright sign of loneliness too great for me,
Strange image of the dread eternity,
In whose void patience how can these have part,
These outstretched feverish hands, this restless heart?

William Morris (1834–1896)

Stars

Alone in the night
  On a dark hill
With pines around me
  Spicy and still,

And a heaven full of stars
  Over my head
White and topaz
  And misty red;

Myriads with beating
  Hearts of fire
That aeons
  Cannot vex or tire;

Up the dome of heaven
  Like a great hill
I watch them marching
  Stately and still.

And I know that I
  Am honored to be
Witness
  Of so much majesty.

Sara Teasdale (1884–1933)

Fibonacci

It must have been around this time of year.
Weathered sheep, white sky, a frozen sun,
snow-hares still flecked with autumn colours,
kites flown from draughty nests. Foxes, long
gone into hiding, let alone by the royal dogs
asleep in Pisa's kennels. Nothing left to ruin
his famous experiment, not the thought
of Geronimo curled in his father's things
through warm Mediterranean nights,
dream-fingers closed on a noiseless toy
made from the tree outside, nor the sense
he finds hard to explain, waking at first light
to a quiet house, of something out of joint,
a pattern unstuck. In the end

what is it that makes him count the pairs?
One afternoon, a sign of nature's genius,
a willow-branch stealing unawares
through the window, stalks of angel's tears
frosted over in their plain geometry?
Or, at forty-seven, the inscrutable
timed tremble in the blood, age's alchemy,
which after a spell turns lead into silver,
then some lighter element? In the mean,

it's said, many seek that constant proof
to which all things must tend, and chance
upon what he alone among them gleans.
Nothing so infinite as to count as truth,
only return, which is a form of consequence.

Theophilus Kwek (1994–)

Childe Harold's Pilgrimage

CANTO THE THIRD

LXXXVIII

Ye stars! which are the poetry of heaven
If in your bright leaves we would read the fate
Of men and empires, – 'tis to be forgiven,
That in our aspirations to be great,
Our destinies o'erleap their mortal state,
And claim a kindred with you; for ye are
A beauty and mystery, and create
In us such love and reverence from afar,
That fortune, fame, power, life, have named themselves a star.

LXXXIX

All heaven and earth are still – though not in sleep,
But breathless, as we grow when feeling most;
And silent, as we stand in thoughts too deep: –
All heaven and earth are still: From the high host
Of stars, to the lull'd lake and mountain-coast,
All is concenter'd in a life intense,
Where not a beam, nor air, nor leaf is lost,
But hath a part of being, and a sense
Of that which is of all Creator and defence.

Lord George Gordon Byron (1788–1824)

10 NOVEMBER

Gradual Clearing

Late in the day the fog
wrung itself out like a sponge
in glades of rain,
sieving the half-invisible
cove with speartips;
then, in a lifting
of wisps and scarves, of smoke-rings
from about the islands, disclosing
what had been wavering
fishnet plissé as a smoothness
of peau-de-soie or just-ironed
percale, with a tatting
of foam out where the rocks are,
the sheened no-color of it,
the bandings of platinum
and magnesium suffusing,
minute by minute, with clandestine
rose and violet, with opaline
nuance of milkweed, a texture
not to be spoken of above a whisper,
began, all along the horizon,
gradually to unseal
like the lip of a cave
or of a cavernous,
single, pearl-
engendering seashell.

Amy Clampitt (1920–1994)

A Hymn in Praise of Neptune

Of Neptune's empire let us sing,
At whose command the waves obey,
To whom the rivers tribute pay,
  Down the high mountains sliding;
To whom the scaly nation yields
Homage for the crystal fields
    Wherein they dwell;
And every sea-god pays a gem,
Yearly out of his watery cell,
To deck the great Neptune's diadem.

The Tritons dancing in a ring
Before his palace gates, do make
The water with their echoes quake,
  Like the great thunder sounding:
The sea-nymphs chant their accents shrill;
  And the Sirens, taught to kill
    With their sweet voice,
Make every echoing rock reply
Unto their gentle murmuring noise
The praise of Neptune's empery.

Thomas Campion (1567–1620)

The Parrot

TRANSLATED BY WILLIAM COWPER

In painted plumes superbly drest,
A native of the gorgeous east,
  By many a billow tost;
Poll gains at length the British shore,
Part of the captain's precious store –
  A present to his toast.

Belinda's maids are soon preferr'd,
To teach him now then a word,
  As Poll can master it;
But 'tis her own important charge,
To qualify him more at large,
  And make him quite a wit.

Sweet Poll! his doating mistress cries,
Sweet Poll! the mimic bird replies,
  And calls aloud for sack.
She next instructs him in the kiss;
'Tis now a little one, like Miss,
  And now a hearty smack.

At first he aims at what he hears;
And, list'ning close with both his ears,
  Just catches at the sound;
But soon articulates aloud,
Much to th' amusement of the crowd,
  And stuns the neighbours round.

A querulous old woman's voice
His hum'rous talent next employs –
  He scolds and gives the lie.
And now he sings, and now is sick –
Here, Sally, Susan, come, come quick,
  Poor Poll is like to die!

Belinda and her bird! 'tis rare
To meet with such a well match'd pair,
  The language and the tone,
Each character in ev'ry part
Sustain'd with so much grace and art,
  And both in unison.

When children first begin to spell,
And stammer out a syllable,
  We think them tedious creatures;
But difficulties soon abate,
When birds are to be taught to prate,
  And women are the teachers.

Vincent Bourne (1695–1747)

The Moon

She comes! again she comes, the bright-eyed moon!
Under a ragged cloud I found her out,
Clasping her own dark orb like hope in doubt!
That ragged cloud hath waited her since noon,
And he hath found and he will hide her soon!
Come, all ye little winds that sit without,
And blow the shining leaves her edge about,
And hold her fast – ye have a pleasant tune!
She will forget us in her walks at night
Among the other worlds that are so fair!
She will forget to look on our despair!
She will forget to be so young and bright!
Nay, gentle moon, thou hast the keys of light –
I saw them hanging by thy girdle there!

George MacDonald (1824–1905)

14 NOVEMBER

Hayeswater Boat

VERSES 1 AND 2

A region desolate and wild.
Black, chafing water: and afloat,
And lonely as a truant child
In a waste wood, a single boat:
No mast, no sails are set thereon;
It moves, but never moveth on:
And welters like a human thing
Amid the wild waves weltering.

Behind, a buried vale doth sleep,
Far down the torrent cleaves its way:
In front the dumb rock rises steep,
A fretted wall of blue and grey;
Of shooting cliff and crumbled stone
With many a wild weed overgrown:
All else, black water: and afloat,
One rood from shore, that single boat.

Matthew Arnold (1822–1888)

At a Lunar Eclipse

Thy shadow, Earth, from Pole to Central Sea,
Now steals along upon the Moon's meek shine
In even monochrome and curving line
Of imperturbable serenity.

How shall I link such sun-cast symmetry
With the torn troubled form I know as thine,
That profile, placid as a brow divine,
With continents of moil and misery?

And can immense Mortality but throw
So small a shade, and Heaven's high human scheme
Be hemmed within the coasts yon arc implies?

Is such the stellar gauge of earthly show,
Nation at war with nation, brains that teem,
Heroes, and women fairer than the skies?

Thomas Hardy (1840–1928)

On Rover, A Lady's Spaniel

ADVICE TO A DOG PAINTER, LINES 1–16

Happiest of the spaniel race,
Painter, with thy colours grace:
Draw his forehead large and high,
Draw his blue and humid eye;
Draw his neck so smooth and round,
Little neck with ribbons bound,
And the muscly swelling breast,
Where the Loves and Graces rest;
And the spreading, even back,
Soft, and sleek, and glossy black;
And the tail that gently twines,
Like the tendrils of the vines;
And the silky twisted hair,
Shadowing thick the velvet ear;
Velvet ears, which, hanging low,
O'er the veiny temples flow.

Jonathan Swift (1667–1745)

November

The lonely season in lonely lands, when fled
Are half the birds, and mists lie low, and the sun
Is rarely seen, nor strayeth far from his bed;
The short days pass unwelcomed one by one.

  Out by the ricks the mantled engine stands
Crestfallen, deserted, – for now all hands
Are told to the plough, – and ere it is dawn appear
The teams following and crossing far and near,
As hour by hour they broaden the brown bands
Of the striped fields; and behind them firk and prance
The heavy rooks, and daws grey-pated dance:
As awhile, surmounting a crest, in sharp outline
(A miniature of toil, a gem's design,)
They are pictured, horses and men, or now near by
Above the lane they shout lifting the share,
By the trim hedgerow bloom'd with purple air;
Where, under the thorns, dead leaves in huddle lie
Packed by the gales of Autumn, and in and out
The small wrens glide
With a happy note of cheer,
And yellow amorets flutter above and about,
Gay, familiar in fear.

And now, if the night shall be cold, across the sky
Linnets and twites, in small flocks helter-skelter,
All the afternoon to the gardens fly,
From thistle-pastures hurrying to gain the shelter
Of American rhododendron or cherry-laurel:
And here and there, near chilly setting of sun,
In an isolated tree a congregation
Of starlings chatter and chide,
Thickset as summer leaves, in garrulous quarrel:
Suddenly they hush as one, –
The tree top springs, –
And off, with a whirr of wings,
They fly by the score
To the holly-thicket, and there with myriads more
Dispute for the roosts; and from the unseen nation
A babel of tongues, like running water unceasing,
Makes live the wood, the flocking cries increasing,
Wrangling discordantly, incessantly,
While falls the night on them self-occupied;
The long dark night, that lengthens slow,
Deepening with Winter to starve grass and tree,
And soon to bury in snow
The Earth, that, sleeping 'neath her frozen stole,
Shall dream a dream crept from the sunless pole
Of how her end shall be.

Robert Bridges (1844–1930)

By the Sea

Why does the sea moan evermore?
  Shut out from heaven it makes its moan,
It frets against the boundary shore;
  All earth's full rivers cannot fill
  The sea, that drinking thirsteth still.

Sheer miracles of loveliness
  Lie hid in its unlooked-on bed:
Anemones, salt, passionless,
  Blow flower-like; just enough alive
  To blow and multiply and thrive.

Shells quaint with curve, or spot, or spike,
  Encrusted live things argus-eyed,
All fair alike, yet all unlike,
  Are born without a pang, and die
  Without a pang, and so pass by.

Christina Rossetti (1830–1894)

To Night

VERSES 1–3

I

Swiftly walk o'er the western wave,
    Spirit of Night!
Out of the misty eastern cave,
Where, all the long and lone daylight,
Thou wovest dreams of joy and fear,
Which make thee terrible and dear, –
    Swift be thy flight!

II

Wrap thy form in a mantle gray,
    Star-inwrought!
Blind with thine hair the eyes of Day;
Kiss her until she be wearied out,
Then wander o'er city, and sea, and land,
Touching all with thine opiate wand –
    Come, long-sought!

III

When I arose and saw the dawn
    I sighed for thee;
When light rode high, and the dew was gone,
And noon lay heavy on flower and tree,
And the weary Day turned to his rest,
Lingering like an unloved guest.
    I sighed for thee.

Percy Bysshe Shelley (1792–1822)

Night of Love

The moon has left the sky, love,
The stars are hiding now,
And frowning on the world, love,
Night bares her sable brow.

The snow is on the ground, love,
And cold and keen the air is.
I'm singing here to you, love;
You're dreaming there in Paris.

But this is Nature's law, love,
Though just it may not seem,
That men should wake to sing, love;
While maidens sleep and dream.

Them care may not molest, love,
Nor stir them from their slumbers,
Though midnight find the swain, love.
Still halting o'er his numbers.

I watch the rosy dawn, love,
Come stealing up the east,
While all things round rejoice, love,
That Night her reign has ceased.

The lark will soon be heard, love,
And on his way be winging;
When Nature's poets, wake, love,
Why should a man be singing?

Paul Laurence Dunbar (1872–1906)

21 NOVEMBER

The Tuft of Kelp

All dripping in tangles green,
  Cast up by a lonely sea
If purer for that, O Weed,
  Bitterer, too, are ye?

Herman Melville (1819–1891)

The Shell

What has the sea swept up?
A Viking oar, long mouldered in the peace
Of grey oblivion? Some dim-burning bowl
Of unmixed gold, from far-off island feasts?
Ropes of old pearls? Masses of ambergris?
Something of elfdom from the ghastly isles
Where white-hot rocks pierce through the flying spindrift?
Or a pale sea-queen, close wound in a net of spells?

Nothing of these. Nothing of antique splendours
That have a weariness about their names:
But – fresh and new, in frail transparency,
Pink as a baby's nail, silky and veined
As a flower petal – this casket of the sea,
One shell.

Mary Webb (1881–1927)

Escape at Bedtime

The lights from the parlour and kitchen shone out
  Through the blinds and the windows and bars;
And high overhead and all moving about,
  There were thousands of millions of stars.
There ne'er were such thousands of leaves on a tree,
  Nor of people in church or the Park,
As the crowds of the stars that looked down upon me,
  And that glittered and winked in the dark.

The Dog, and the Plough, and the Hunter, and all,
  And the star of the sailor, and Mars,
These shone in the sky, and the pail by the wall
  Would be half full of water and stars.
They saw me at last, and they chased me with cries,
  And they soon had me packed into bed;
But the glory kept shining and bright in my eyes,
  And the stars going round in my head.

Robert Louis Stevenson (1850–1894)

Once We Were Wolves

dashing like smoke through silvered firs.
Our eyes were hurtling moons in the violence
of night, affixed upon our prey of hare and hart.
Our bodies were frosted pine needles, the shadowy
grace of fear. Our paws made the silent tread
not of feet but of rampant years. Our muzzles
described scree-paved landslides, and our fangs
were the jagged treetops in misty midnight.
Our tails, meanwhile, saluted heaven like our
looning cries. We had wilderness for comfort,
the hunt for our joy, and the rain that found us
stirred the taste of earth from beneath our claws.

Adam Lowe (1985–)

25 NOVEMBER

Twilight

The stately tragedy of dusk
  Drew to its perfect close,
The virginal white evening star
  Sank and the red moon rose.

Sara Teasdale (1884–1933)

26 NOVEMBER

Gulf

with pale determination we stood either
side of the gulf, hair quite salt-
stung, a metallic taste in our mouths.

breath poised.

then the gulf widened, its perimeter
was lost & into that breach
poured the wind: a night wind that could
not recall day's passing.

Joel Knight (1975–)

The Last Walk in Autumn

VERSES 1–3

I

O'er the bare woods, whose outstretched hands
  Plead with the leaden heavens in vain,
I see, beyond the valley lands,
  The sea's long level dim with rain.
Around me all things, stark and dumb,
Seem praying for the snows to come,
And, for the summer bloom and greenness gone,
With winter's sunset lights and dazzling morn atone.

II

Along the river's summer walk,
  The withered tufts of asters nod;
And trembles on its arid stalk
  The boar plume of the golden-rod.
And on a ground of sombre fir,
And azure-studded juniper,
The silver birch its buds of purple shows,
And scarlet berries tell where bloomed the sweet wild-rose!

III

With mingled sound of horns and bells,
   A far-heard clang, the wild geese fly,
Storm-sent, from Arctic moors and fells,
   Like a great arrow through the sky,
Two dusky lines converged in one,
Chasing the southward-flying sun;
While the brave snow-bird and the hardy jay
Call to them from the pines, as if to bid them stay.

John Greenleaf Whittier (1807–1892)

The Cormorant

Now the seagull spreads his wing,
And the puffin seeks the shore,
Home flies every living thing,
Yo, ho! the breakers roar!
  Only the Cormorant, dark and sly,
  Watches the waves with a sea-green eye.

Under his bows the breakers fleet,
All alone, alone went he;
Flying alone through the blinding sleet.
Flying alone through the raging sea.
  Only the Cormorant, dark and sly,
  Watches the waves with a sea-green eye.

Round his bark the billows roar,
Dancing along to a lonely grave;
Death behind, and Death before
Yo, ho! the breakers rave!
  Only the Cormorant, dark and sly,
  Watches the waves with a sea-green eye.

Hark! the waves on their iron floor,
See Kilstiffin's naked brow!
Iron cliff, and iron shore,
Erin's saints preserve him now!
  Only the Cormorant, dark and sly,
  Watches the waves with a sea-green eye.

Hark! was that a drowing cry?
Erin's saints receive his soul!
Nothing now twixt sea and sky
Yo, ho! the breakers roll!
  Only the Cormorant, dark and sly,
  Watches the waves with a sea-green eye.

Emily Lawless (1845–1913)

A Winter Piece

LINES 1–27

The time has been that these wild solitudes,
Yet beautiful as wild – were trod by me
Oftener than now; and when the ills of life
Had chafed my spirit – when the unsteady pulse
Beat with strange flutterings – I would wander forth
And seek the woods. The sunshine on my path
Was to me as a friend. The swelling hills,
The quiet dells retiring far between,
With gentle invitation to explore
Their windings, were a calm society
That talked with me and soothed me. Then the chant
Of birds, and chime of brooks, and soft caress
Of the fresh sylvan air, made me forget
The thoughts that broke my peace, and I began
To gather simples by the fountain's brink,
And lose myself in day-dreams. While I stood
In nature's loneliness, I was with one
With whom I early grew familiar, one
Who never had a frown for me, whose voice
Never rebuked me for the hours I stole
From cares I loved not, but of which the world
Deems highest, to converse with her. When shrieked

The bleak November winds, and smote the woods,
And the brown fields were herbless, and the shades,
That met above the merry rivulet,
Were spoiled, I sought, I loved them still, – they seemed
Like old companions in adversity.

William Cullen Bryant (1794–1878)

30 NOVEMBER

11 The Sea

I concede – I don't know what this feeling is,
like dolphins tripping over dominoes.

It's easy to recognise honesty
from an airplane over the Atlantic.

Astronauts are wiser than we are,
While you sleep in a light that's already past.

I wish to be different
but under skylights and mud roofs,

space is a rearview mirror.
The truth about sunshine

kids learn early.
Half a daydream.

In the park you wear my denim jacket
and diplomatic love.

In their whiteness and coupleness
the other couples are silent

like bobbin lace.
Under the red imperial pavilion,

it rains to bring us together.

Kandace Siobhan-Walker

DECEMBER

A Silence Deep and White

First Day of Winter

Like the bloom on a grape is the evening air
And a first faint frost the wind has bound.
Yet the fear of his breath avails to scare
The withered leaves on the cold ground.

For they huddle and whisper in phantom throngs,
I hear them beneath the branches bare:
We danced with the Wind, we sang his songs;
Now he pursues us, we know not where.

Laurence Binyon (1869–1943)

The Induction

VERSES 1–3

The wrathful winter, 'proaching on apace,
  With blustering blasts had all ybared the treen,
And old Saturnus, with his frosty face,
  With chilling cold had pierced the tender green;
  The mantles rent, wherein enwrapped been
    The gladsome groves that now lay overthrown,
    The tapets torn, and every bloom down blown.

The soil, that erst so seemly was to seen,
  Was all despoiled of her beauty's hue;
And soote fresh flowers, wherewith the summer's queen
  Had clad the earth, now Boreas' blasts down blew;
  And small fowls flocking, in their song did rue
    The winter's wrath, wherewith each thing defaced
    In woeful wise bewailed the summer past.

Hawthorn had lost his motley livery,
  The naked twigs were shivering all for cold,
And dropping down the tears abundantly;
  Each thing, methought, with weeping eye me told
  The cruel season, bidding me withhold
    Myself within; for I was gotten out
    Into the fields, whereas I walked about.

Thomas Sackville (1536–1608)

The Moon was but a Chin of Gold

The Moon was but a Chin of Gold
A Night or two ago –
And now she turns Her perfect Face
Upon the World below –

Her Forehead is of Amplest Blonde -
Her Cheek – a Beryl hewn –
Her Eye unto the Summer Dew
The likest I have known -–

Her Lips of Amber never part –
But what must be the smile
Upon Her Friend she could confer
Were such Her Silver Will –

And what a privilege to be
But the remotest Star –
For Certainty She take Her Way
Beside Your Palace Door –

Her Bonnet is the Firmament –
The Universe – Her Shoe –
The Stars – the Trinkets at Her Belt –
Her Dimities –of Blue –

Emily Dickinson (1830–1886)

The Retired Cat

A poet's cat, sedate and grave
As poet well could wish to have,
Was much addicted to inquire
For nooks, to which she might retire,
And where, secure as mouse in chink,
She might repose, or sit and think.
I know not where she caught the trick –
Nature perhaps herself had cast her
In such a mould PHILOSOPHIQUE,
Or else she learn'd it of her master.
Sometimes ascending, debonair,
An apple-tree or lofty pear,
Lodg'd with convenience in the fork,
She watched the gard'ner at his work;
Sometimes her ease and solace sought
In an old empty wat'ring-pot,
There, wanting nothing save a fan,
To seem some nymph in her sedan,
Apparell'd in exactest sort,
And ready to be borne to court.
  But love of change, it seems, has place
Not only in our wiser race;
Cats also feel as well as we
That passion's force, and so did she.
Her climbing, she began to find,
Expos'd her too much to the wind,
And the old utensil of tin

Was cold and comfortless within:
She therefore wish'd instead of those
Some place of more serene repose,
Where neither cold might come, nor air
Too rudely wanton with her hair,
And sought it in the likeliest mode
Within her master's snug abode.
All if poss, cut here if necessary
  A draw'r, – it chanc'd, at bottom lin'd
With linen of the softest kind,
With such as merchants introduce
From India, for the ladies' use, –
A draw'r impending o'er the rest,
Half-open in the topmost chest,
Of depth enough, and none to spare,
Invited her to slumber there;
Puss with delight beyond expression
Survey'd the scene, and took possession.
Recumbent at her ease ere long,
And lull'd by her own hum-drum song,
She left the cares of life behind,
And slept as she would sleep her last,
When in came, housewifely inclin'd,
The chambermaid, and shut it fast,
By no malignity impell'd,
But all unconscious whom it held.
  Awaken'd by the shock (cried puss)
Was ever cat attended thus!

The open draw'r was left, I see,
Merely to prove a nest for me.
For soon as I was well compos'd,
Then came the maid, and it was closed:
How smooth these 'kerchiefs, and how sweet,
O what a delicate retreat!
I will resign myself to rest
Till Sol, declining in the west,
Shall call to supper; when, no doubt,
Susan will come and let me out.
  The evening came, the sun descended,
And puss remain'd still unattended.
The night roll'd tardily away,
(With her indeed 'twas never day)
The sprightly morn her course renew'd,
The evening gray again ensued,
And puss came into mind no more
Than if entomb'd the day before.
With hunger pinch'd, and pinch'd for room,
She now presag'd approaching doom,
Nor slept a single wink, or purr'd,
Conscious of jeopardy incurr'd.
  That night, by chance, the poet watching
Heard an inexplicable scratching,
His noble heart went pit-a-pat
And to himself he said – what's that?
He drew the curtain at his side,
And forth he peep'd, but nothing spied.

Yet, by his ear directed, guess'd
Something imprison'd in the chest,
And doubtful what, with prudent care
Resolv'd it should continue there.
At length a voice which well he knew,
A long and melancholy mew,
Saluting his poetic ears,
Consol'd him, and dispell'd his fears;
He left his bed, he trod the floor,
He 'gan in haste the draw'rs explore,
The lowest first, and without stop,
The rest in order to the top;
For 'tis a truth well known to most,
That whatsoever thing is lost,
We seek it, ere it come to light,
In ev'ry cranny but the right.
Forth skipp'd the cat; not now replete
As erst with airy self-conceit,
Nor in her own fond apprehension,
A theme for all the world's attention,
But modest, sober, cur'd of all
Her notions hyperbolical,
And wishing for a place of rest
Any thing rather than a chest.
Then stept the poet into bed,
With this reflexion in his head:

MORAL

Beware of too sublime a sense
Of your own worth and consequence!
The man who dreams himself so great,
And his importance of such weight,
That all around, in all that's done
Must move and act for him alone,
Will learn, in school of tribulation
The folly of his expectation.

William Cowper (1731–1800)

Nightpiece

Gaunt in gloom,
The pale stars their torches,
Enshrouded, wave.
Ghostfires from heaven's far verges faint illume,
Arches on soaring arches,
Night's sindark nave.

Seraphim,
The lost hosts awaken
To service till
In moonless gloom each lapses muted, dim,
Raised when she has and shaken
Her thurible.

And long and loud,
To night's nave upsoaring,
A starknell tolls
As the bleak incense surges, cloud on cloud,
Voidward from the adoring
Waste of souls.

James Joyce (1882–1941)

Winter-Time

Late lies the wintry sun a-bed,
A frosty, fiery sleepy-head;
Blinks but an hour or two; and then,
A blood-red orange, sets again.

Before the stars have left the skies,
At morning in the dark I rise;
And shivering in my nakedness,
By the cold candle, bathe and dress.

Close by the jolly fire I sit
To warm my frozen bones a bit;
Or with a reindeer-sled, explore
The colder countries round the door.

When to go out, my nurse doth wrap
Me in my comforter and cap;
The cold wind burns my face, and blows
Its frosty pepper up my nose.

Black are my steps on silver sod;
Thick blows my frosty breath abroad;
And tree and house, and hill and lake,
Are frosted like a wedding-cake.

Robert Louis Stevenson (1850–1894)

A Beech

They will not go. These leaves insist on staying.
Coinage like theirs looked frail six weeks ago.
What hintings at, excitement of delaying,
Almost as if some richer fruits could grow

If leaves hung on against each swipe of storm,
If branches bent but still did not give way.
Today is brushed with sun. The leaves are warm.
I picked one from the pavement and it lay

With borrowed shining on my Winter hand.
Persistence of this nature sends the pulse
Beating more rapidly. When will it end,

That pride of leaves? When will the branches be
Utterly bare, and seem like something else,
Now half-forgotten, no part of a tree?

Elizabeth Jennings (1926–2001)

General Description

FROM *THE BOROUGH*, LINES 194–213

View now the winter-storm! above, one cloud,
Black and unbroken, all the skies o'ershroud:
Th' unwieldy porpoise through the day before
Had roll'd in view of boding men on shore;
And sometimes hid and sometimes show'd his form,
Dark as the cloud, and furious as the storm.
All where the eye delights, yet dreads to roam,
The breaking billows cast the flying foam
Upon the billows rising – all the deep
Is restless change; the waves so swell'd and steep,
Breaking and sinking, and the sunken swells,
Nor one, one moment, in its station dwells:
But nearer land you may the billows trace,
As if contending in their watery chase;
May watch the mightiest till the shoal they reach,
Then break and hurry to their utmost stretch;
Curl'd as they come, they strike with furious force,
And then re-flowing, take their grating course,
Raking the rounded flints, which ages past
Roll'd by their rage, and shall to ages last.

George Crabbe (1754–1832)

Frost at Midnight

LINES 1–16

The Frost performs its secret ministry,
Unhelped by any wind. The owlet's cry
Came loud – and hark, again! loud as before.
The inmates of my cottage, all at rest,
Have left me to that solitude, which suits
Abtruser musings: save that at my side
My cradled infant slumbers peacefully.
'Tis calm indeed! so calm, that it disturbs
And vexes meditation with its strange
And extreme stillness. Sea, hill, and wood,
This populous village! Sea, and hill, and wood,
With all the numberless goings-on of life,
Inaudible as dreams! the thin blue flame
Lies on my low-burnt fire, and quivers not;
Only that film, which fluttered on the grate,
Still flutters there, the sole unquiet thing.

Samuel Taylor Coleridge (1772–1834)

Stopping by Woods on a Snowy Evening

Whose woods these are I think I know.
His house is in the village though;
He will not see me stopping here
To watch his woods fill up with snow.

My little horse must think it queer
To stop without a farmhouse near
Between the woods and frozen lake
The darkest evening of the year.

He gives his harness bells a shake
To ask if there is some mistake.
The only other sound's the sweep
Of easy wind and downy flake.

The woods are lovely, dark and deep,
But I have promises to keep,
And miles to go before I sleep.
And miles to go before I sleep.

Robert Frost (1874–1963)

Earth to Earth

VERSES 1 AND 2

Where the region grows without a lord,
  Between the thickets emerald-stoled,
In the woodland bottom the virgin sward,
  The cream of the earth, through depths of mold
    O'erflowing wells from secret cells,
While the moon and the sun keep watch and ward,
And the ancient world is never old.

Here, alone, by the grass-green hearth
  Tarry a little: the mood will come!
Feel your body a part of earth;
  Rest and quicken your thought at home;
    Take your ease with the brooding trees;
Join in their deep-down silent mirth
  The crumbling rock and the fertile loam.

John Davidson (1857–1909)

Trees

The Oak is called the king of trees,
The Aspen quivers in the breeze,
The Poplar grows up straight and tall,
The Peach-tree spreads along the wall,
The Sycamore gives pleasant shade,
The Willow droops in watery glade,
The Fir-tree useful timber gives,
The Beech amid the Forest lives.

Sara Coleridge (1802–1852)

How still, how happy!

How still, how happy! Those are words
That once would scarce agree together;
I loved the plashing of the surge –
The changing heaven the breezy weather,

More than smooth seas and cloudless skies
And solemn, soothing, softened airs
That in the forest woke no sighs
And from the green spray shook no tears.

How still, how happy! Now I feel
Where silence dwells is sweeter far
Than laughing mirth's most joyous swell
However pure its raptures are.

Come, sit down on this sunny stone:
'Tis wintry light o'er flowerless moors –
But sit – for we are all alone
And clear expand heaven's breathless shores.

I could think in the withered grass
Spring's budding wreaths we might discern;
The violet's eye might shyly flash
And young leaves shoot among the fern.

It is but thought – full many a night
The snow shall clothe those hills afar
And storms shall add a drearier blight
And winds shall wage a wilder war,

Before the lark may herald in
Fresh foliage twined with blossoms fair
And summer days again begin
Their glory-haloed crown to wear.

Yet my heart loves December's smile
As much as July's golden beam;
Then let us sit and watch the while
The blue ice curdling on the stream.

Emily Brontë (1818–1848)

The First Snow-Fall

VERSES 1–4

The snow had begun in the gloaming,
And busily all the night
Had been heaping field and highway
With a silence deep and white.

Every pine and fir and hemlock
Wore ermine too dear for an earl,
And the poorest twig on the elm-tree
Was ridged inch deep with pearl.

From sheds new-roofed with Carrara
Came Chanticleer's muffled crow,
The stiff rails softened to swan's-down,
And still fluttered down the snow.

I stood and watched by the window
The noiseless work of the sky,
And the sudden flurries of snowbirds,
Like brown leaves whirling by.

James Russell Lowell (1819–1891)

A December Day

Dawn turned on her purple pillow
  And late, late came the winter day,
Snow was curved to the boughs of the willow.
  The sunless world was white and grey.

At noon we heard a blue-jay scolding,
  At five the last thin light was lost
From snow-banked windows faintly holding
  The feathery filigree of frost.

Sara Teasdale (1884–1933)

Winter's Beauty

Is it not fine to walk in spring,
When leaves are born, and hear birds sing?
And when they lose their singing powers,
In summer, watch the bees at flowers?
Is it not fine, when summer's past,
To have the leaves, no longer fast,
Biting my heel where'er I go,
Or dancing lightly on my toe?
Now winter's here and rivers freeze;
As I walk out I see the trees,
Wherein the pretty squirrels sleep,
All standing in the snow so deep:
And every twig, however small,
Is blossomed white and beautiful.
Then welcome, winter, with thy power
To make this tree a big white flower;
To make this tree a lovely sight,
With fifty brown arms draped in white,
While thousands of small fingers show
In soft white gloves of purest snow.

W. H. Davies (1871–1940)

17 DECEMBER

The Winter Evening

THE TASK, BOOK IV, LINES 311–332

I saw the woods and fields, at close of day,
A variegated show; the meadows green,
Though faded; and the lands, where lately wav'd
The golden harvest, of a mellow brown,
Upturn'd so lately by the forceful share.
I saw far off the weedy fallows smile
With verdure not unprofitable, graz'd
By flocks, fast-feeding, and selecting each
His fav'rite herb; while all the leafless groves,
That skirt th' horizon, wore a sable hue,
Scarce notic'd in the kindred dusk of eve.
To-morrow brings a change, a total change!
Which even now, though silently perform'd,
And slowly, and by most unfelt, the face
Of universal nature undergoes.
Fast falls a fleecy show'r: the downy flakes,
Descending, and with never-ceasing lapse,
Softly alighting upon all below,
Assimilate all objects. Earth receives
Gladly the thick'ning mantle; and the green
And tender blade that fear'd the chilling blast,
Escapes unhurt beneath so warm a veil.

William Cowper (1731–1800)

Stars Sliding

The stars are sliding wanton through trees,
  The sky is sliding steady over all.
Great Bear to Gemini will lose his place
  And Cygnus over world's brink slip and fall.

Follow-my-Leader's not so bad a game.
  But were it Leap Frog: O! to see the shoots
And tracks of glory; Scorpions and Swans tame
  And Argo swarmed with Bulls and other brutes.

Ivor Gurney (1890–1937)

19 DECEMBER

To the Evening Star

VERSES 1–4

Gem of the crimson-colour'd Even,
Companion of retiring day,
Why at the closing gates of heaven,
Beloved Star, dost thou delay?

So fair thy pensile beauty burns
When soft the tear of twilight flows;
So due thy plighted love returns
To chambers brighter than the rose;

To Peace, to Pleasure, and to Love
So kind a star thou seem'st to be,
Sure some enamour'd orb above
Descends and burns to meet with thee!

Thine is the breathing, blushing hour
When all unheavenly passions fly,
Chased by the soul-subduing power
Of Love's delicious witchery.

Thomas Campbell (1777–1844)

There Was a Boy

There was a boy – ye knew him well, ye cliffs
And islands of Winander – many a time
At evening, when the stars had just begun
To move along the edges of the hills,
Rising or setting, would he stand alone
Beneath the trees or by the glimmering lake,
And there, with fingers interwoven, both hands
Pressed closely palm to palm and to his mouth
Uplifted, he, as though an instrument,
Blew mimic hootings to the silent owls,
That they might answer him. And they would shout
Across the watery vale, and shout again,
Responsive to his call, with quavering peals,
And long halloos, and screams, and echoes loud,
Redoubled and redoubled – a wild scene
Of mirth and jocund din. And when it chanced
That pauses of deep silence mocked his skill,
Then sometimes in that silence, while he hung
Listening, a gentle shock of mild surprise
Has carried far into his heart the voice
Of mountain torrents; or the visible scene
Would enter unawares into his mind
With all its solemn imagery – its rocks,
Its woods, and that uncertain heaven – received
Into the bosom of the steady lake.

William Wordsworth (1770–1850)

21 DECEMBER

Moon Haze

Because the moonlight deceives
Therefore I love it.

Amy Lowell (1874–1925)

Childe Harold's Pilgrimage

CANTO THE FOURTH

CLXXVIII

There is a pleasure in the pathless woods,
There is a rapture on the lonely shore,
There is society, where none intrudes,
By the deep Sea, and music in its roar:
I love not Man the less, but Nature more,
From these our interviews, in which I steal
From all I may be, or have been before,
To mingle with the Universe, and feel
What I can ne'er express, yet cannot all conceal.

Lord George Gordon Byron (1788–1824)

Through Springtime Walks

Through springtime walks, with flowers perfumed,
  I chased a wild capricious fair,
Where hyacinths and jonquils bloomed,
  Chanting gay sonnets through the air;
    Hid amid a briary dell
      Or 'neath a hawthorn-tree,
    Her sweet enchantments led me on
      And still deluded me.

While summer's 'splendent glory smiles
  My ardent love in vain essayed,
I strove to win her heart by wiles,
  But still a thousand pranks she played;
Still o'er each sunburnt furzy hill,
  Wild, playful, gay, and free,
She laughed and scorned; I chased her still,
  And still she bantered me.

When autumn waves her golden ears
  And wafts o'er fruits her pregnant breath,
The sprightly lark its pinions rears;
  I chased her o'er the daisied heath,
And all around was glee –
Still, wanton as the timid hart,
  She swiftly flew from me.

Now winter lights its cheerful fire,
  While jests with frolic mirth resound
And draws the wandering beauty nigher,
  'Tis now too cold to rove around;
The Christmas-game, the playful dance,
  Incline her heart to glee –
Mutual we glow, and kindling love
  Draws every wish to me.

Ann Batten Cristall (1769-1848)

Arracombe Wood

Some said, because he wud'n spaik
Any words to women but Yes and No,
Nor put out his hand for Parson to shake
He mun be bird-witted. But I do go
By the lie of the barley that he did sow,
And I wish for no better thing than to hold a rake
Like Dave, in his time, or to see him mow.

Put up in the churchyard a month ago,
'A bitter old soul,' they said, but it wadn't so.
His heart were in Arracombe Wood where he'd used to go
To sit and talk wi' his shadder till sun went low,
Thought what it was all about us'll never know.
And thee baint no mem'ry in the place
Of th' old man's footmark, nor his face;
Arracombe Wood do think more of a crow –
'Will be violets there in the Spring: in Summer time the spider's lace;
And come the Fall, the whizzle and race
Of the dry, dead leaves when the wind gies chase;
And on the Eve of Christmas, fallin' snow.

Charlotte Mew (1869–1928)

Christmas Night

Softly, softly, through the darkness
  Snow is falling.
Sharply, sharply, in the meadows
  Lambs are calling.
Coldly, coldly, all around me
  Winds are blowing.
Brightly, brightly, up above me
  Stars are glowing.

Anon

Winter Trees on the Horizon

O delicate! Even in wooded lands
  They show the margin of my world,
My own horizon; little bands
  Of twigs unveil that edge impearled,

And what is more mine own than this –
  My limit, level with mine eyes?
For me precisely do they kiss –
  The rounded earth, the rounding skies.

It has my stature, that keen line
  (Let mathematics vouch for it).
The lark's horizon is not mine,
  No, nor his nestlings' where they sit;

No, nor the child's. And, when I gain
  The hills, I lift it as I rise
Erect; anon, back to the plain
  I soothe it with mine equal eyes.

Alice Meynell (1847–1922)

Rose-berries

The green pine-needles shiver glassily,
Each cased in ice. Harsh winter, grey and dun,
Shuts out the sun.
But with live, scarlet fire,
Enfolding seed of sweet Junes yet to be,
Rose-berries melt the snow, and burn above
The thorny briar,
Like beauty with its deathless seed of love.

Mary Webb (1881–1927)

Winter Branches

Against the smoke-browned wall
The browner winter branches
Stand out hardly at all;
They do not tremble in the misty evening.

But under the open sky
Where the stars in clear and tranquil
Sufficiency go by,
They leap up quivering into the vastness

Like flame, like the thought of man
Leaping from earth's nurture,
Through span on alien span,
To tremble around the stars its kindred.

Nan Shepherd (1893–1981)

The Cat

Within that porch, across the way,
  I see two naked eyes this night;
Two eyes that neither shut nor blink,
  Searching my face with a green light.

But cats to me are strange, so strange –
  I cannot sleep if one is near;
And though I'm sure I see those eyes,
  I'm not so sure a body's there!

W. H. Davies (1871–1940)

Snowbound: A Winter Idyl, 1865

LINES 1–18

The sun that brief December day
Rose cheerless over hills of gray,
And, darkly circled, gave at noon
A sadder light than waning moon.
Slow tracing down the thickening sky
Its mute and ominous prophecy,
A portent seeming less than threat,
It sank from sight before it set.
A chill no coat, however stout,
Of homespun stuff could quite shut out,
A hard, dull bitterness of cold,
  That checked, mid-vein, the circling race
  Of life-blood in the sharpened face,
The coming of the snow-storm told.
The wind blew east; we heard the roar
Of Ocean on his wintry shore,
And felt the strong pulse throbbing there
Beat with low rhythm our inland air.

John Greenleaf Whittier (1807–1892)

The Darkling Thrush

I leant upon a coppice gate
  When Frost was spectre-gray,
And Winter's dregs made desolate
  The weakening eye of day.
The tangled bine-stems scored the sky
  Like strings of broken lyres,
And all mankind that haunted nigh
  Had sought their household fires.

The land's sharp features seemed to be
  The Century's corpse outleant,
His crypt the cloudy canopy,
  The wind his death-lament.
The ancient pulse of germ and birth
  Was shrunken hard and dry,
And every spirit upon earth
  Seemed fervourless as I.

At once a voice arose among
  The bleak twigs overhead
In a full-hearted evensong
  Of joy illimited;
An aged thrush, frail, gaunt, and small,
  In blast-beruffled plume,
Had chosen thus to fling his soul
  Upon the growing gloom.

So little cause for carolings
  Of such ecstatic sound
Was written on terrestrial things
  Afar or nigh around,
That I could think there trembled through
  His happy good-night air
Some blessed Hope, whereof he knew
  And I was unaware.

Thomas Hardy (1840–1928)

Index of First Lines

Index of Poets

Acknowledgements

Jason Allen-Paisant, 'Tree Dreaming', *More Fiyah* (2021), Canongate. Copyright: © Jason Allen-Paisant 2022

W H Auden, 'Dog and Cat', from *Collected Shorter Poems 1927-1957*. Reprinted by permission of Curtis Brown, Ltd.

David Austin, 'Winter Trees', 'A Flower of the Himalayas', 'The Sea by Moonlight', and 'Soil', from *The Breathing Earth*, Enitharmon Press, 2014. Reprinted with permission of David Austin Roses.

Patricia Beer, 'The Estuary', from *Patricia Beer: Collected Poems*, Carcanet Press, 1990. Reprinted by permission of Carcanet Press Limited.

John Betjeman, 'Diary of a Church Mouse', from *John Betjeman Collected Poems*, John Murray Press. © The Estate of John Betjeman 1955, 1958, 1960, 1962, 1964,1966, 1970, 1979, 1980, 1981, 2001. Introduction Andrew Motion © 2006. Reproduced by permission of John Murray Publishers, an imprint of Hodder and Stoughton Limited.

Edmund Blunden, 'Spring Night' and 'A Waterpiece', from Edmund Blunden: Selected Poems, Carcanet Press, 1982. Reprinted by permission of Carcanet Press Limited.

Amy Clampitt, 'Gradual Clearing' from *The Collected Poems of Amy Clampitt* © 1997 by the Estate of Amy Clampitt. Used by permission of Alfred A. Knopf, an imprint of the Knopf Doubleday Publishing Group, a division of Penguin Random House LLC. All rights reserved.

Shastra Deo, 'A Boar Buys Real Estate in Fukushima

Prefecture' is from *The Uncollected Animals: Poems for Our Nonhuman Kin, A Global Anthology*. Copyright © 2026 by Shastra Deo. Reprinted by permission of Turtle Point Press.

Patrick Dickinson, 'Bluebells', from *Poets of Our Time*, J. Murray, 1965. Reprinted with permission of Penguin Random House.

Rita Dove, 'Dawn Revisited', from ON THE BUS WITH ROSA PARKS by Rita Dove. Copyright © 1999 by Rita Dove. Used by permission of W. W. Norton & Company, Inc.

Clifford Dyment, 'The King of the Wood', from *Experiences and Places*, J M Dent, 1955.

T S Eliot, 'Little Giddings', from *Four Quartets*, Faber & Faber, 2001. Reprinted with permission of Faber & Faber.

Eleanor Farjeon, 'March, You Old Blusterer' and 'Night-piece', from *The Children's Bells*, Oxford University Press, 1973. Reprinted by kind permission of David Higham Associates Ltd.

John Foster, 'The Lake' and 'Kingfisher', from *The Poetry Chest*, Oxford University Press, 2007. Reproduced with permission of the Licensor through PLSclear.

Robert Frost, 'The Road Not Taken' and 'Stopping by Woods on a Snowy Evening', from *The Complete Poems*, Cape, 1951. Reprinted with permission of Penguin Random House.

Ted Hughes, 'The Harvest Moon', from *New Selected Poems*

1957-1994, Faber & Faber, 1995. Reprinted with permission of Faber & Faber.

Elizabeth Jennings, 'Beech', from *Collected Poems of Elizabeth Jennings 1953-1985*, Carcanet, 1986. Reprinted by kind permission of David Higham Associates Ltd.

Joel Knight, 'Night', 'No Matter', 'Gulf'. With kind permission of Joel Knight.

Theophilus Kwek, 'Fibonacci', *The First Five Thunderstorms* (2017) Smith | Doorstop.

Philip Larkin, 'The Trees', from High Windows, Faber & Faber, 2003. Reprinted with permission of Faber & Faber.

Laurie Lee, 'Field of Autumn'. Reproduced with permission of Curtis Brown Group Ltd, London on behalf of The Beneficiary of the Estate of Laurie Lee. Copyright © Laurie Lee, 1947.

Adam Lowe, 'Once We Were Wolves' from *More Fiyah* (2021), Canongate, © Adam Lowe.

Edna St Vincent Millay, 'Renascence' and 'God's World', from *The selected Poetry of Edna St Vincent Millay*, Nancy Milford, Modern Library Torchbearers, 2002.

Iris Murdoch, 'October', from *A Year of Birds*. Reproduced with permission of Curtis Brown Group Ltd, London on behalf of The Estate of Iris Murdoch. Copyright © Iris Murdoch, 1978.

Walter de la Mare, 'A Robin' and 'Silver', from *Walter de la Mare Selected Poems*, Faber & Faber, 2006. 'Echo', from

Collected Rhymes and Verses, Faber & Faber, 1944. Courtesy of The Society of Authors.

Alice Oswald, 'Snowdrop', from *Weeds and Wild Flowers*, Alice Oswald, Faber & Faber, 2009. Reprinted with permission of United Agents.

Mavis Pilbeam, 'Sounds in the Wood', from *Birds*, British Museum Press, 2015. Reprinted with permission of Mavis Pilbeam.

Nan Shepherd, 'Winter Branches', from *In the Cairngorms*, Galileo Publishing, 2014. Reprinted with permission of Galileo Publishing.

Vita Sackville-West, 'Autumn', from *The Land*, Francis Lincoln, 1989. Reprinted with permission of Penguin Random House.

Kandace Siobhan-Walker, '11 The Sea', *Kaleido* (2022), Bad Betty Press.

Andrew Young, 'Winter Morning' and 'The Mountain', from *The Poetical Works*, Carcanet Press. Reprinted by permission of Carcanet Press Limited.

As always, a huge thanks to everyone at Hatchards for looking after my books so well. Thanks to Jeremy Bourne for recommending poems, Joel Knight for writing them and the staff at The Saison Poetry Library on the South Bank in London and The Scottish Poetry Library just off the Canongate in Edinburgh for all their help. Nicola Newman, Tina Persaud and Lilly Phelan at Batsford were consistently wonderful editors and Teresa Chris my agent has been as supportive as ever. Lastly, for the curious readers, Matilda is a small grey tabby cat, who went missing for three months whilst I was compiling this anthology. Without Mat and Sarah it would have been a much harder time. Happily she was rescued and has resumed her duties as my paperweight.